myWorld TEXAS Social Studies®

Here We Are

PEARSON

Boston, Massachusetts • Chandler, Arizona • Glenview, Illinois • New York, New York

It's my story, too!

You are one of the authors of this book. You can write in this book! You can take notes in this book! You can draw in it, too! This book will be yours to keep.

Fill in the information below.

Name

School

City or Town

Front: Top: Monarch butterfly; **Second Row:** Statue of Liberty; **Third Row:** L: Subway shuttle in Dallas; C: United States flag; R: Soccer ball; **Bottom:** Turtle swimming in the Gulf of Mexico, off Texas

Back: Top: Small town, U.S.A.; **Center:** C: Firefighter; **R:** United States penny; **Bottom:** L: Crossing guard helping children on their way to school; **R:** A map that helps us find places

Credits appear on page **R4,** which constitutes an extension of this copyright page.

PEARSON

Softcover: ISBN-13: 978-0-328-81349-0
ISBN-10: 0-328-81349-4
8 9 10 V003 18 17 16

Hardcover: ISBN-13: 978-0-328-84903-1
ISBN-10: 0-328-84903-0
3 4 5 6 7 8 9 10 V003 19 18 17 16 15

Built for Texas

Pearson *Texas myWorld Social Studies* was developed especially for Texas with the help of teachers from across the state and covers 100 percent of the Texas Essential Knowledge and Skills for Social Studies. This story began with a series of teacher roundtables in cities across the state of Texas that inspired a program blueprint for *Texas myWorld Social Studies*. In addition, Judy Brodigan served as our expert advisor, guiding our creation of a dynamic Social Studies curriculum for TEKS mastery. Once this blueprint was finalized, a dedicated team—made up of Pearson authors, content experts, and social studies teachers from Texas—worked to bring our collective vision into reality.

Pearson would like to extend a special thank you to all of the teachers who helped guide the development of this program. We gratefully acknowledge your efforts to realize the possibilities of elementary Social Studies teaching and learning. Together, we will prepare Texas students for their future roles in college, careers, and as active citizens.

Program Consulting Authors

The Colonial Williamsburg Foundation
Williamsburg VA

Armando Cantú Alonzo
Associate Professor of History
Texas A&M University
College Station TX

Dr. Linda Bennett
Associate Professor, Department of Learning, Teaching, & Curriculum
College of Education
University of Missouri
Columbia MO

Dr. James B. Kracht
Byrne Chair for Student Success
Executive Associate Dean
College of Education and Human Development
College of Education
Texas A&M University
College Station TX

Dr. William E. White
Vice President for Productions, Publications and Learning Ventures
The Colonial Williamsburg Foundation
Williamsburg VA

Padre Island National Seashore

Reviewers and Consultants

ACADEMIC REVIEWERS

Kathy Glass
Author, *Lesson Design for Differentiated Instruction*
President, Glass Educational Consulting
Woodside CA

Roberta Logan
African Studies Specialist
Retired, Boston Public Schools/ Mission Hill School
Boston MA

Jeanette Menendez
Reading Coach
Doral Academy Elementary
Miami FL

Bob Sandman
Adjunct Assistant Professor of Business and Economics
Wilmington College—Cincinnati Branches
Blue Ash OH

PROGRAM CONSULTANT

Judy Brodigan
Former President, Texas Council for Social Studies
Grapevine TX

Celebrating Texas and the Nation

Chapter 1 My Family, My School

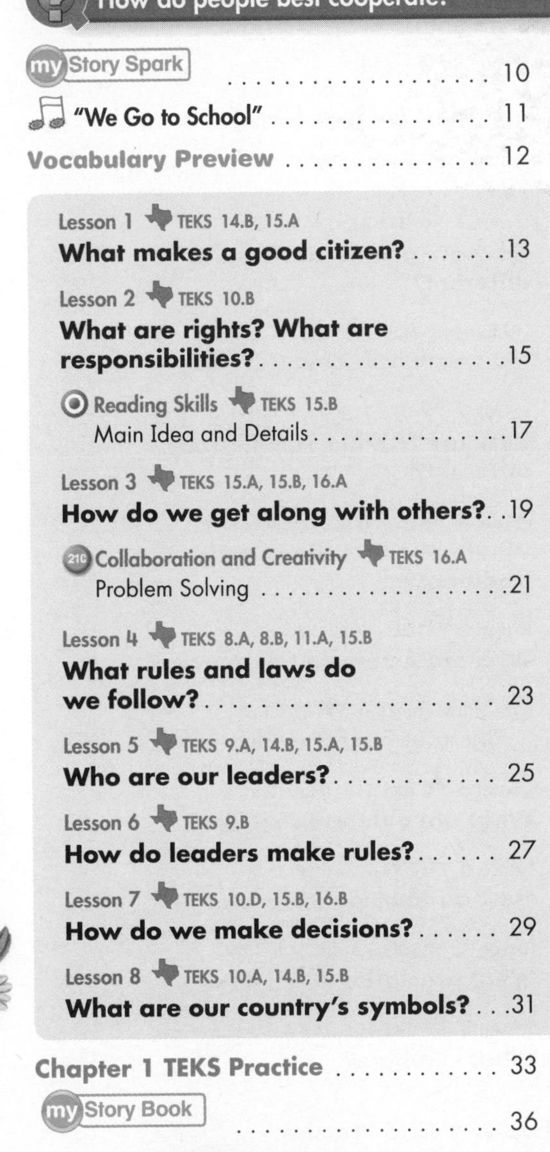

The Big Question: How do people best cooperate?

Chapter 2 Everybody Works

The Big Question: How do people get what they need?

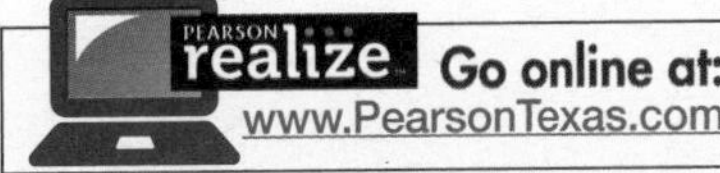

Go online at: www.PearsonTexas.com

Every chapter is supported by digital presentations, myStory Videos, vocabulary activities, songs, and myStory Book on Tikatok.

Chapter 3
Where We Live

The Big ? What is the world like?

Chapter 4
Our Traditions

The Big ? How is culture shared?

Chapter 5
Life Then and Now

The Big ? How does life change throughout history?

Celebrating Texas and the Nation

Texas Essential Knowledge and Skills

10.C Identify Constitution Day as a celebration of American freedom.

Celebrate Freedom

What is freedom?

Freedom is the right to make choices.

We choose where we live and play.

We celebrate freedom!

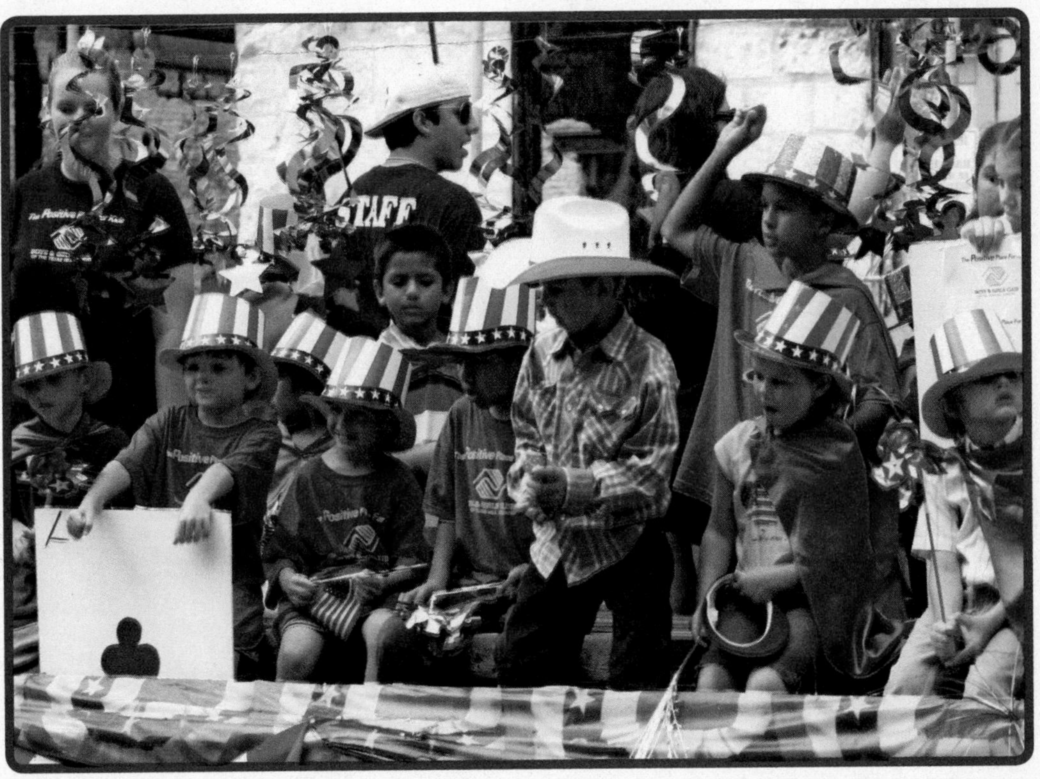

Teaching Note: Read the text aloud. Discuss what the people in the picture are doing. Explain that people in the United States have the freedom to make choices. We can choose where we live, work, go to school, and play. Encourage children to talk about what they are free to do each day at home, at school, and in their community. Discuss why freedom is important to us and how we celebrate freedom.

Celebrate Freedom

What is Constitution Day?

We celebrate Constitution Day on September 17.
We remember our rules and laws.

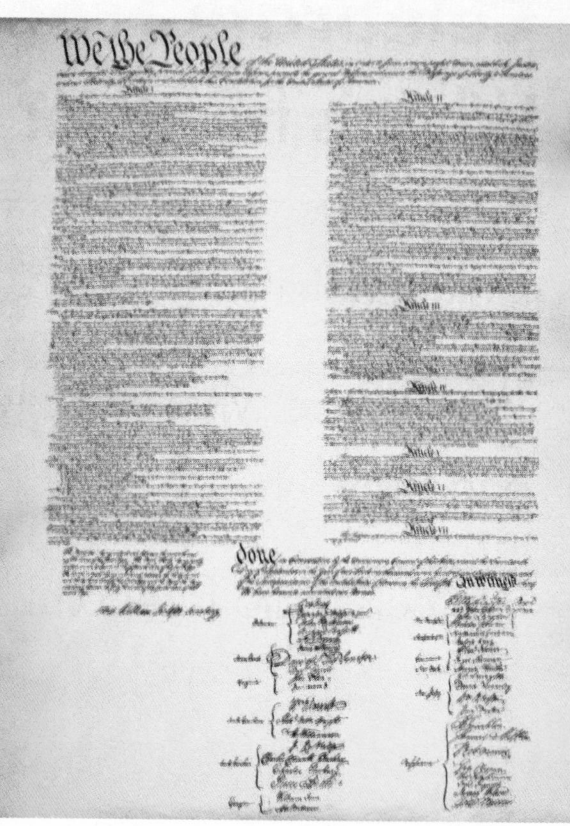

Draw a picture.

Show how you celebrate Constitution Day.

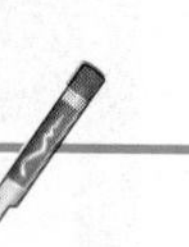

Teaching Note: Explain that more than 200 years ago leaders made a plan for rules and laws when our country became free. Point to the U.S. Constitution. Say that it ensures freedom for all. Explain that we celebrate freedom and our "book of rules and laws" on September 17. We also honor our leaders from long ago who wrote the laws. Discuss activities children do on Constitution Day. After children complete the activity, ask them to tell about their pictures.

Celebrate Freedom

What does freedom mean to me?

Draw a picture. **Show** what freedom means to you.

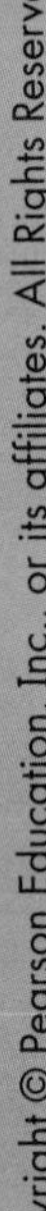

Teaching Note: Remind children that we have the freedom to choose where we live, work, go to school, and play. Discuss what it would mean if we couldn't make these choices. Then invite children to draw a picture that shows what freedom means to them. Encourage children to include activities that are important to them, such as playing with friends, celebrating a special day in the community, or going on a school field trip.

Texas Essential Knowledge and Skills

2.A Identify contributions of historical figures, including Stephen F. Austin, George Washington, Christopher Columbus, and José Antonio Navarro, who helped to shape the state and nation.

2.B Identify contributions of patriots and good citizens who have shaped the community.

Who are Texas heroes?

Heroes work to help other people.

Heroes work to help their state, too.

Teaching Note: Read the text aloud. Help children identify the person in each picture. Tell how Austin and Navarro were citizens who contributed to Texas and its communities. Explain that Austin brought many families to settle in Texas and that people call him the Father of Texas. Navarro wanted freedom for Texas and signed an important paper called the Texas Declaration of Independence. Discuss how both men were heroes and patriots.

Who are Texas heroes?

Circle a picture of a Texas hero from the past.

Tell the hero's story.

Teaching Note: Point out to children that the pictures on this page show the same people as on the first page of the lesson. Have children circle one picture. Then help them retell that person's story. Encourage children to tell why he was a patriot and citizen who contributed to Texas and its communities. Ask them why they chose that particular person.

Texas Essential Knowledge and Skills

10.A Identify the flags of the United States and Texas.
10.B Recite the Pledge of Allegiance to the United States Flag and the Pledge to the Texas Flag.

What is the United States flag?

The flag is a symbol of our country.
We say a pledge to the flag.

Draw a picture.
Show how you honor the United States flag.

Teaching Note: Read the text aloud. Point to the flag. Explain that this important patriotic symbol has 50 stars, and that each star stands for one of the 50 states, including Texas. Discuss why we say the Pledge of Allegiance to the United States flag. Tell children that a pledge is a promise to be loyal. Invite children to stand and face the flag. Help them recite the pledge. After children complete the activity, invite them to tell about their pictures.

Celebrating Texas and the Nation

Texas Essential Knowledge and Skills

10.A Identify the flags of the United States and Texas.
10.B Recite the Pledge of Allegiance to the United States Flag and the Pledge to the Texas Flag.

What is the Texas flag?

The flag is a symbol of our state.

We say a pledge to the flag.

Draw a picture of the Texas flag.

Tell why you say a pledge to it.

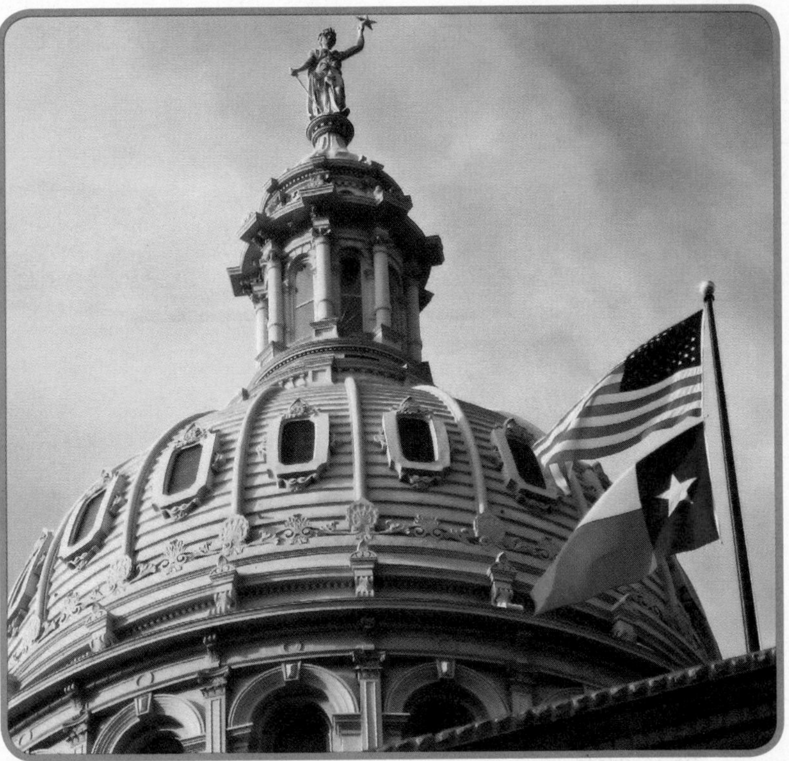

Teaching Note: Point to the Texas flag in the picture. Explain that it is sometimes called "The Lone Star Flag" because of the flag's one white star. Discuss the similarities to and differences from the United States flag. Explain that this patriotic symbol stands for loyalty and that when we say a pledge to it, we promise to show that we care about our state. Help children recite the Pledge to the Texas flag. Ask them to tell why it is important to show respect to the flag.

Texas Essential Knowledge and Skills

14.A Obtain information about a topic using a variety of valid oral sources such as conversations, interviews, and music.

"Texas, Our Texas"

Sing this song. **Show** you care about your state.
Tell why you care about it, too.

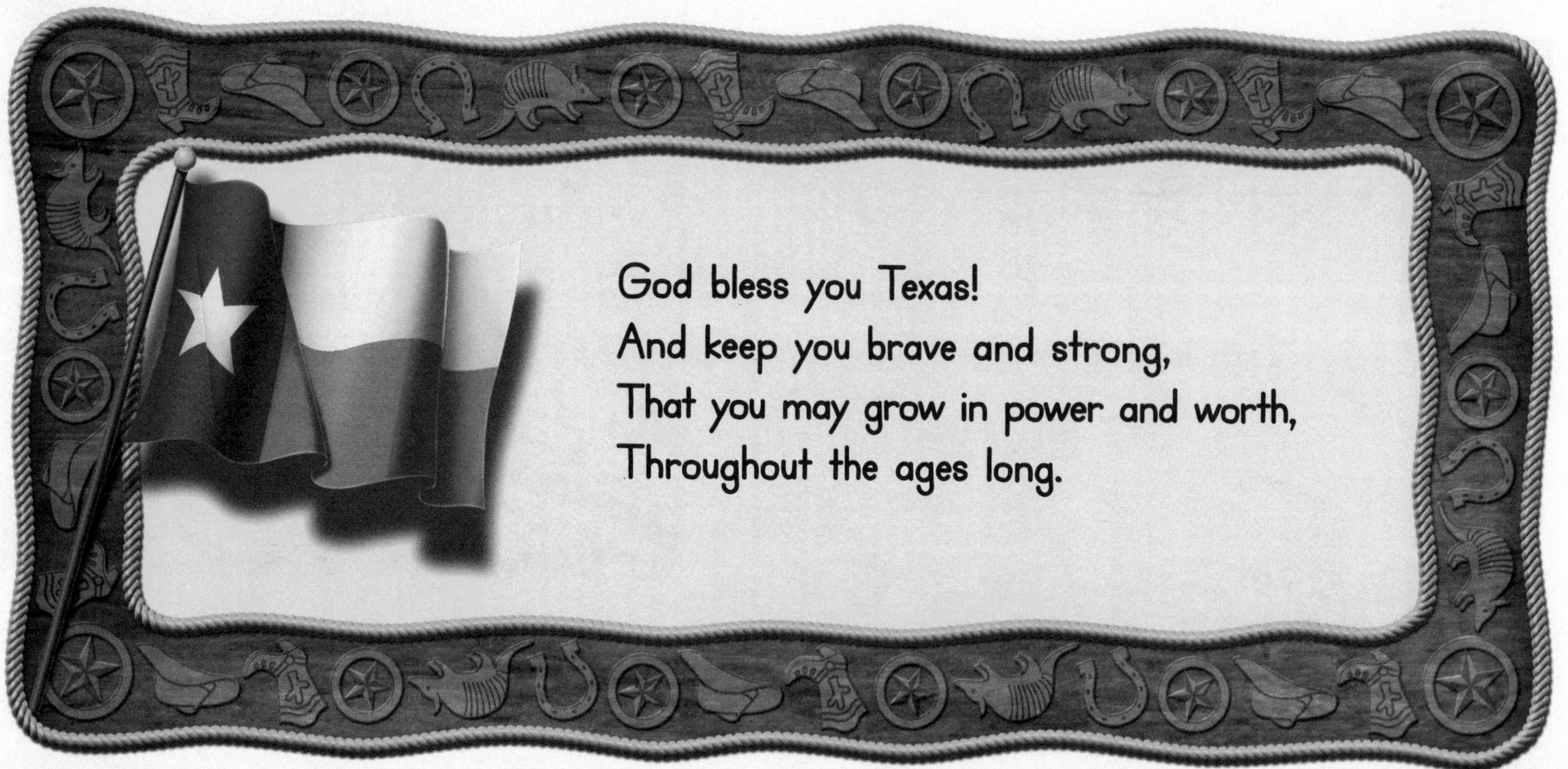

God bless you Texas!
And keep you brave and strong,
That you may grow in power and worth,
Throughout the ages long.

Teaching Note: Explain that one way we show that we care about Texas is to sing songs that honor it. Say each line of the song, and encourage children to repeat it. When they are comfortable, sing the song and invite children to chime in when they are able. Then encourage children to tell why they care about their state.

Texas

Chapter

1

My Family, My School

THE BIG ? How do people best cooperate?

Teaching Note: Explain that *cooperate* means to "work together." Discuss how the children in the photo work together to carry the large American flag. Ask what might happen if the children in the photo did not cooperate or work together well.

PEARSON realize Go online to access your interactive digital lesson.

Chapter 1

My Family, My School

Texas Essential Knowledge and Skills

15.B Create and interpret visuals, including pictures and maps.

my Story Spark

Draw a picture of yourself working with a friend.

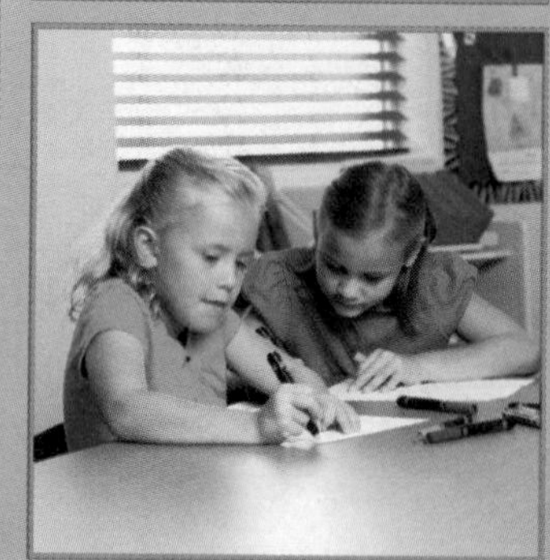

Teaching Note: Discuss ways children can work together to do a school project or a classroom job. Use the photos on the page for ideas. Then read the prompt aloud. Explain that people can create pictures to tell a story without words. Tell children to put details in their pictures to tell their stories.

Begin With a Song

Texas Essential Knowledge and Skills

14.A Obtain information about a topic using a variety of valid oral sources such as conversations, interviews, and music.

We Go to School

Sing to the tune of "The Farmer in the Dell."

We go to school each day.
We learn in every way.
We learn to read
And write and spell.
We learn to work and play.

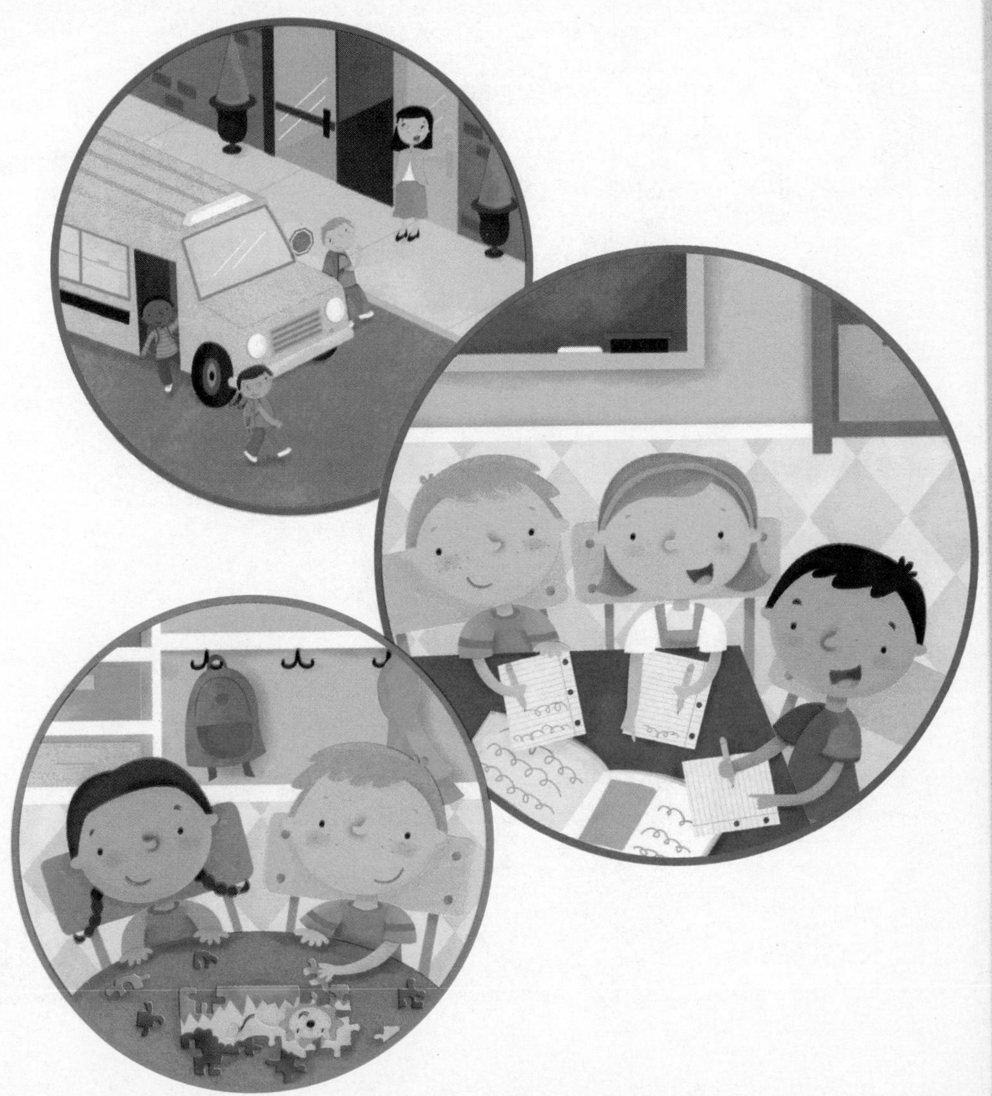

Teaching Note: Sing the song as you point to the picture that goes with each part. Then have children point to the pictures as you sing the song together. Ask what other activities they do in school each day.

PEARSON realize Go online to access your interactive digital lesson.

Chapter 1

Vocabulary Preview

Circle examples of these words in the picture.

citizen

school

leader

FRANKLIN SCHOOL

rule

symbol

cooperate

Teaching Note: Point to the small photos as you read the words aloud. Use additional examples to define each word. Then tour the central picture with children and discuss the scene. Say each vocabulary word, and assist children as needed in circling an example in the picture.

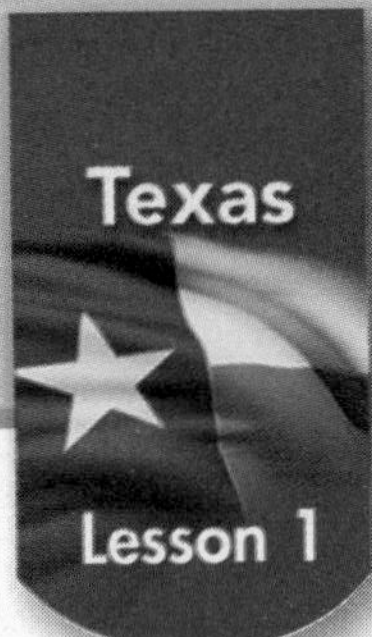

What makes a good citizen?

Texas Essential Knowledge and Skills

14.B Obtain information about a topic using a variety of valid visual sources such as pictures, symbols, electronic media, print material, and artifacts.

15.A Express ideas orally based on knowledge and experiences.

I can help. I can take turns.

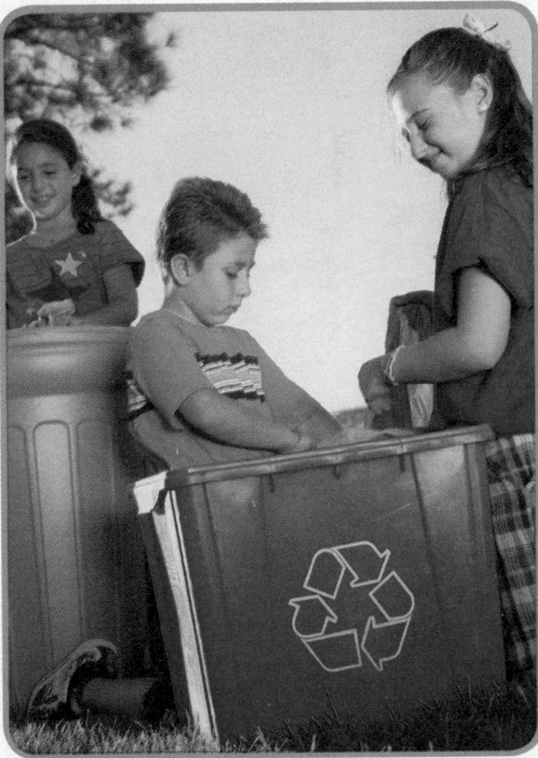

Teaching Note: Explain that good citizens care about their country, their community, and other people. As you discuss the photos and text, brainstorm ways that children can demonstrate good citizenship.

PEARSON realize Go online to access your interactive digital lesson.

Texas

Lesson 1

What makes a good citizen?

Texas Essential Knowledge and Skills

14.B Obtain information about a topic using a variety of valid visual sources such as pictures, symbols, electronic media, print material, and artifacts.

15.A Express ideas orally based on knowledge and experiences.

Tell how these children are good citizens.

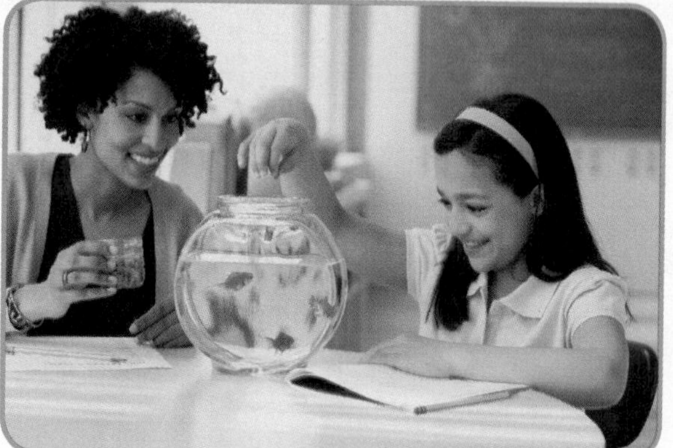

Teaching Note: Read the prompt aloud. Discuss different ways people can demonstrate good citizenship. Talk about how the people in the photos are good citizens. Then have children tell an additional example of how they can be good citizens.

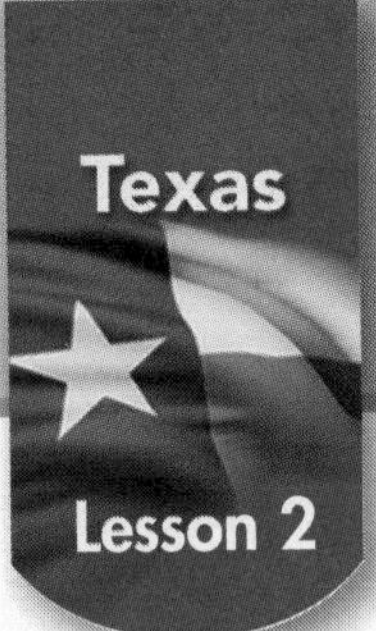

What are rights? What are responsibilities?

Texas Essential Knowledge and Skills

10.B Recite the Pledge of Allegiance to the United States flag and the Pledge to the Texas flag.

I live in a home.
I help my family.

I go to school.
I care about my country.

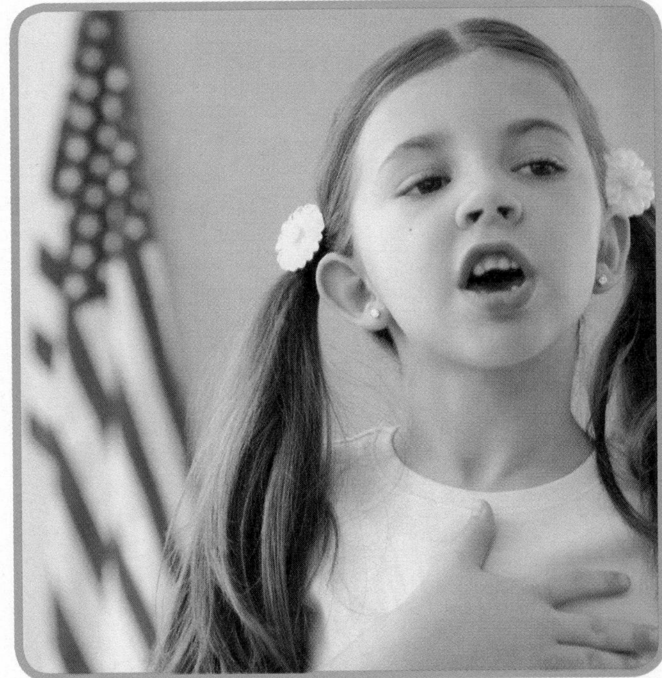

Teaching Note: Help children understand the meaning of *rights*. Explain that children have the right to a home and to go to school. Do the same for *responsibilities*. Discuss home and school responsibilities. Talk about what it means to show you care about your country. Help children recite the Pledge of Allegiance to the United States flag.

What are rights? What are responsibilities?

 **Texas Essential Knowledge and Skills**

10.B Recite the Pledge of Allegiance to the United States flag and the Pledge to the Texas flag.

Draw pictures. **Show** how you help and care.

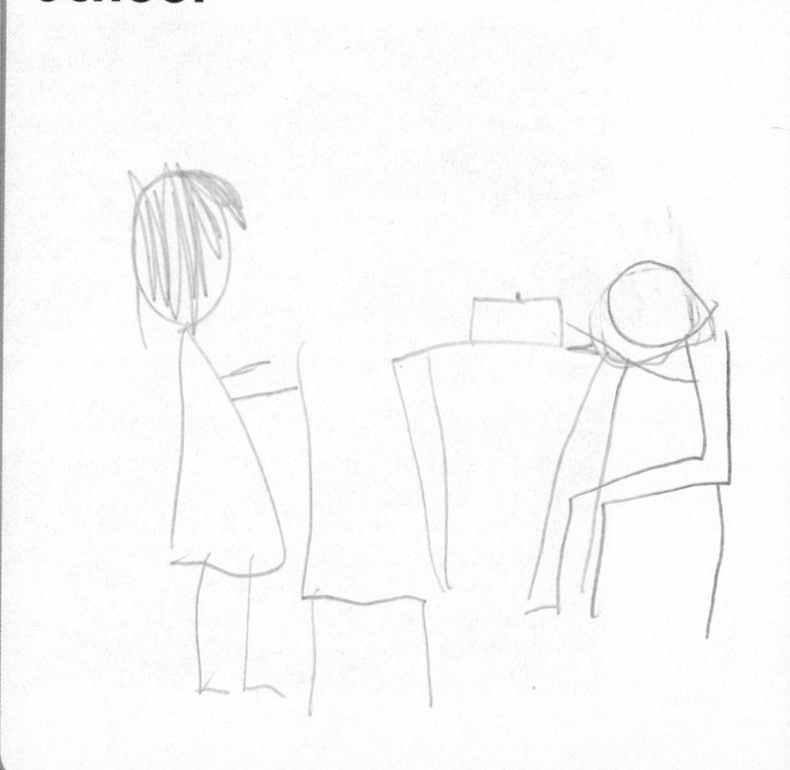

Teaching Note: Read the prompt. Brainstorm different responsibilities children have at home and at school. Write down the answers and read them together. Then have children draw ways they help or care at home and at school, including reciting the Pledge of Allegiance to the flag. Invite them to describe their final pictures.

Reading Skills: Main Idea and Details

TEKS

SS 15.B Interpret visuals, including pictures.

ELA 10.A Identify the topic and details in expository text, referring to the words and illustrations.

The main idea tells what a story is about. The details tell more about the main idea.

<u>Anna and Ben go to school.</u>

They help each other read.

They share toys.

They clean up, too.

main idea

detail

detail

detail

Teaching Note: Read the text aloud. Discuss which sentence tells what the story is about. Point out how the picture labeled "Main Idea" illustrates the underlined sentence. Then reread the details of what Anna and Ben do in school. Have children point to the picture that illustrates each detail.

PEARSON realize. Go online to access your interactive digital lesson.

Reading Skills: Main Idea and Details

TEKS

SS 15.B Interpret visuals, including pictures.
ELA 10.A Identify the topic and details in expository text, referring to the words and illustrations.

Try it!

Underline the main idea.

Lin takes care of Barker.
She gives him a bath.
She feeds him.
Lin takes Barker for a walk, too.

Write "d" under the details.

main idea

Teaching Note: Read the story aloud. Have children identify and underline the main idea. Then reread the details of how Lin takes care of Barker. As you read each one, have children write "d" under the corresponding picture.

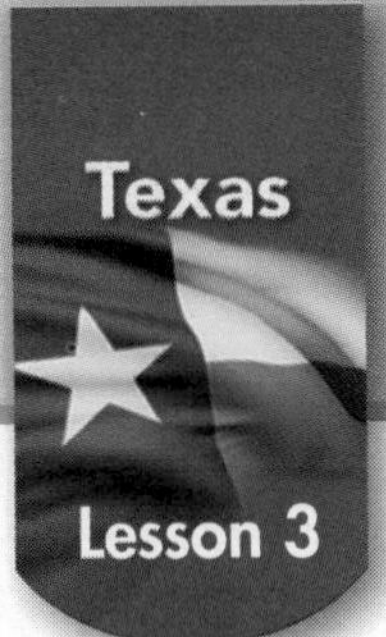

How do we get along with others?

Texas Essential Knowledge and Skills

15.A Express ideas orally based on knowledge and experiences.
15.B Create and interpret visuals, including pictures and maps.
16.A The student uses a problem-solving process to identify a problem, gather information, list and consider options, consider advantages and disadvantages, choose and implement a solution, and evaluate the effectiveness of the solution.

Look at the children at the swing. What is the problem?

How did they solve the problem?

Teaching Note: Cover the picture on the right. Point to the picture on the left and ask children to name the problem. Discuss what else they might need to know about it. Have them think about ways to solve it, and pick one way. Uncover the picture on the right. Discuss how the girls solved the problem and how well their solution worked.

Go online to access your interactive digital lesson.

How do we get along with others?

Texas Essential Knowledge and Skills

15.A Express ideas orally based on knowledge and experiences.
15.B Create and interpret visuals, including pictures and maps.
16.A The student uses a problem-solving process to identify a problem, gather information, list and consider options, consider advantages and disadvantages, choose and implement a solution, and evaluate the effectiveness of the solution.

Look at the children at school.
Tell about the problem.

Draw a picture to solve it.
Tell about your picture.

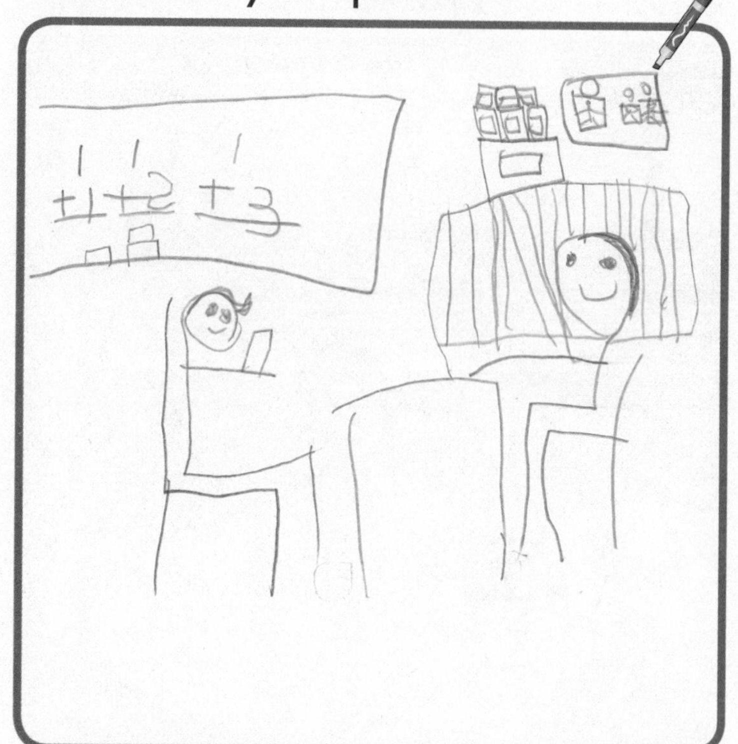

Teaching Note: Read the prompts aloud. Ask children to name the problem and say how they could find out more about it. Have children suggest ways to solve the problem, and then have them make a plan. Encourage children to draw a picture to solve the problem, and then discuss how well their ideas work.

21C

Collaboration and Creativity: Problem Solving

TEKS

SS 16.A Use a problem-solving process to identify a problem, gather information, list and consider options, consider advantages and disadvantages, choose and implement a solution, and evaluate the effectiveness of the solution.

1. Name the problem.
2. Find out about it.
3. Think about ways to solve it.
4. Make a plan.
5. Solve the problem.
6. Think about how your idea worked.

Teaching Note: Read and discuss the first four numbered steps. Then have children look at the large picture on the left. Guide them to name the problem, and suggest ways to solve it. Then point to the smaller picture on the right, and ask how the children solved the problem. Discuss how well this idea would work to solve the problem.

PEARSON realize — Go online to access your interactive digital lesson.

21C

Collaboration and Creativity: Problem Solving

TEKS

SS 16.A Use a problem-solving process to identify a problem, gather information, list and consider options, consider advantages and disadvantages, choose and implement a solution, and evaluate the effectiveness of the solution.

Try it!

1. **Name** the problem.

2. **Circle** the best way to solve the problem.

Teaching Note: Point to the picture on the left, and ask children to name the problem. Encourage them to tell the steps they would take to solve it. Then discuss the three possible solutions pictured. Ask children which is the fairest way to solve the problem so that everyone pictured can do the activity.

Texas

Lesson 4

What rules and laws do we follow?

Texas Essential Knowledge and Skills

8.A Identify purposes for having rules.

8.B Identify rules that provide order, security, and safety in the home and school.

11.A Identify similarities and differences among people such as kinship, laws, and religion.

15.B Create and interpret visuals, including pictures and maps.

Good citizens follow rules.
Good citizens follow laws, too.

home

school

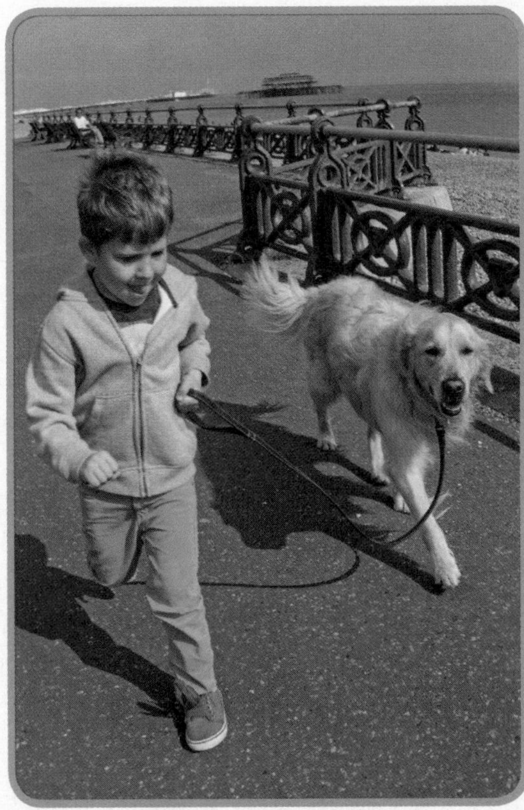

community

Teaching Note: Explain that rules and laws tell us what to do to be good citizens. Discuss reasons for rules and laws, such as keeping people safe and providing order and security at home and in school. Point to the community picture. Explain that some communities have similar laws, while other communities have different ones, such as leash laws.

Go online to access your interactive digital lesson.

Texas

Lesson 4

What rules and laws do we follow?

Texas Essential Knowledge and Skills

8.A Identify purposes for having rules.

8.B Identify rules that provide order, security, and safety in the home and school.

11.A Identify similarities and differences among people such as kinship, laws, and religion.

15.B Create and interpret visuals, including pictures and maps.

Circle people who follow rules and laws.

Teaching Note: Talk about what each person in the picture is doing. Help children circle the people who are following rules and laws. Have children help you make a list of rules and laws that provide order, security, and safety in the home, school, and community. Discuss similarities and differences in community laws.

Texas
Lesson 5

Who are our leaders?

Texas Essential Knowledge and Skills

9.A Identify authority figures in the home, school, and community.
14.B Obtain information about a topic using a variety of valid visual sources such as pictures, symbols, electronic media, print material, and artifacts.
15.A Express ideas orally based on knowledge and experiences.
15.B Create and interpret visuals, including pictures and maps.

Leaders help us in many ways.
They help our community, too.

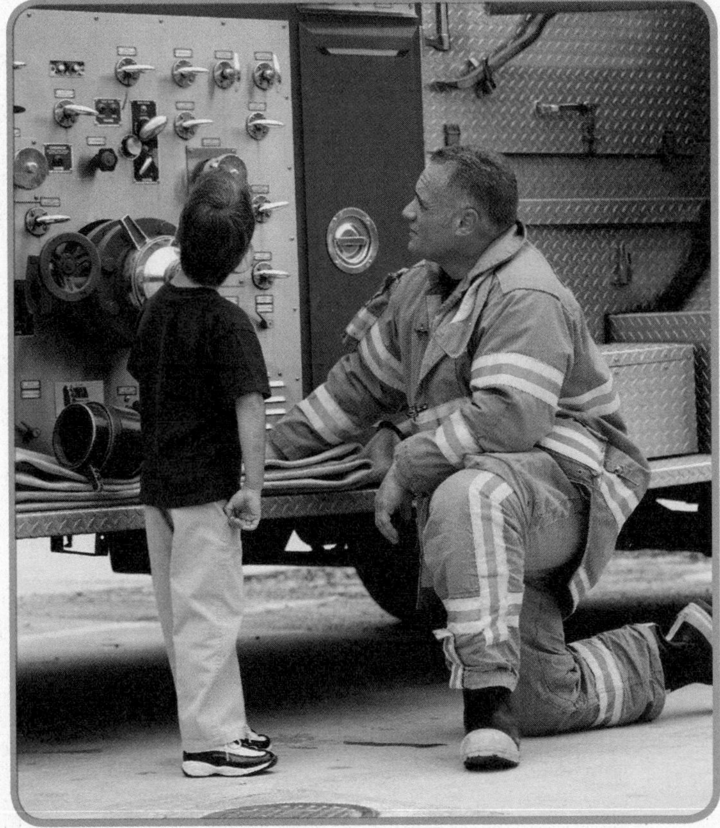

Teaching Note: Ask how a parent is helping as a leader in the photo on the left and how a firefighter is helping as a leader in the photo on the right. Explain that these good citizens help shape their community. Point out that they protect children and keep them safe. Also discuss how school leaders help children.

Go online to access your interactive digital lesson.

Who are our leaders?

Texas Essential Knowledge and Skills

9.A Identify authority figures in the home, school, and community.

14.B Obtain information about a topic using a variety of valid visual sources such as pictures, symbols, electronic media, print material, and artifacts.

15.A Express ideas orally based on knowledge and experiences.

15.B Create and interpret visuals, including pictures and maps.

Name a leader. **Tell** how the leader helps us and our community.

Teaching Note: Assist children in naming the community leader in each photo as a teacher, a doctor or nurse, a librarian, and a crossing guard. Discuss how each leader may help children follow rules and obey laws. Then have children tell how these leaders and others help children in the home, school, and community.

Texas

Lesson 6

How do leaders make rules?

Texas Essential Knowledge and Skills

9.B Explain how authority figures make and enforce rules.

Some leaders make rules. Other leaders make sure we follow rules.

Ms. Lee's Classroom Rules

- Raise your hand.
- Please listen.
- Share books and toys.
- Wash your hands before eating.
- Line up quietly.

Teaching Note: Read the text aloud. Then talk about the photo. Explain how a teacher makes and enforces rules to keep children safe and healthy and to provide order. Point to the rules and read them aloud. Ask what rules the children are following. Brainstorm other rules that children think would be helpful.

Go online to access your interactive digital lesson.

How do leaders make rules?

Texas Essential Knowledge and Skills

9.B Explain how authority figures make and enforce rules.

Name a leader. **Tell** how the leader makes rules or helps us follow them.

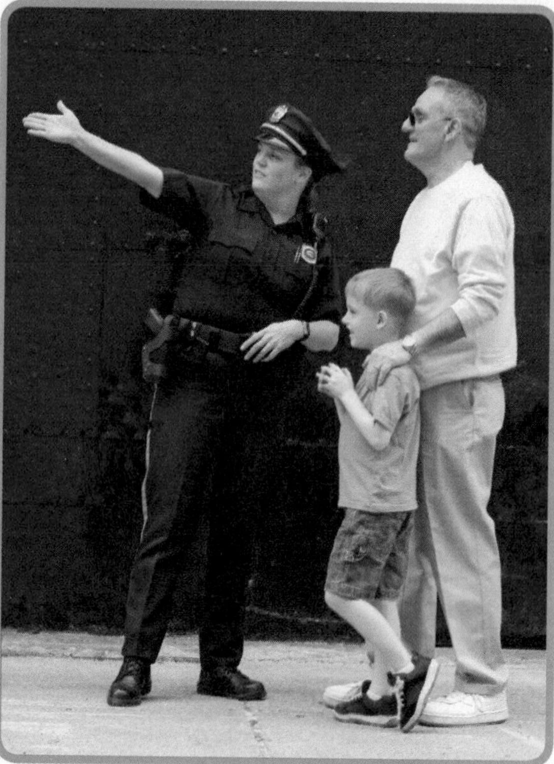

Teaching Note: Assist children in naming the leader in each photo as a parent or caregiver, a principal or teacher, and a police officer. Discuss how each leader makes or enforces rules. Then ask how each leader helps children follow home, school, and community rules and laws.

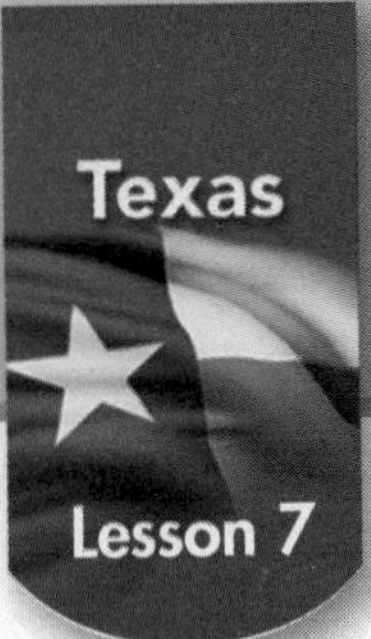

How do we make decisions?

Texas Essential Knowledge and Skills

10.D Use voting as a method for group decision making.
15.B Create and interpret visuals, including pictures and maps.
16.B Use a decision-making process to identify a situation that requires a decision, gather information, generate options, predict outcomes, take action to implement a decision, and reflect on the effectiveness of the decision.

1. Tell about a decision to make.
2. Find out about it.
3. Name choices.
4. Think about each choice.
5. Make a decision.
6. Think about how your decision works.

Teaching Note: Define *decision* as making a choice between two or more things. Have children look at the large picture. Read the steps. Discuss how the mom and son can use them to make a decision. Then look at the smaller picture. Discuss voting as a way groups can make decisions. Have children raise hands to vote on a class activity.

Go online to access your interactive digital lesson.

Texas

Lesson 7

How do we make decisions?

Texas Essential Knowledge and Skills

10.D Use voting as a method for group decision making.
15.B Create and interpret visuals, including pictures and maps.
16.B Use a decision-making process to identify a situation that requires a decision, gather information, generate options, predict outcomes, take action to implement a decision, and reflect on the effectiveness of the decision.

Draw one way you make a decision with friends.

Teaching Note: Read the prompt. Talk about why friends may need to make a decision, such as to choose an activity. Then review ways friends may make a decision, such as by voting about what to do. Encourage children to describe the decision-making process in their drawings.

Texas

Lesson 8

What are our country's symbols?

Texas Essential Knowledge and Skills

10.A Identify the flags of the United States and Texas.
14.B Obtain information about a topic using a variety of valid visual sources such as pictures, symbols, electronic media, print material, and artifacts.
15.B Create and interpret visuals, including pictures and maps.

Symbols are important.
These symbols stand for the United States.
They stand for freedom, too.

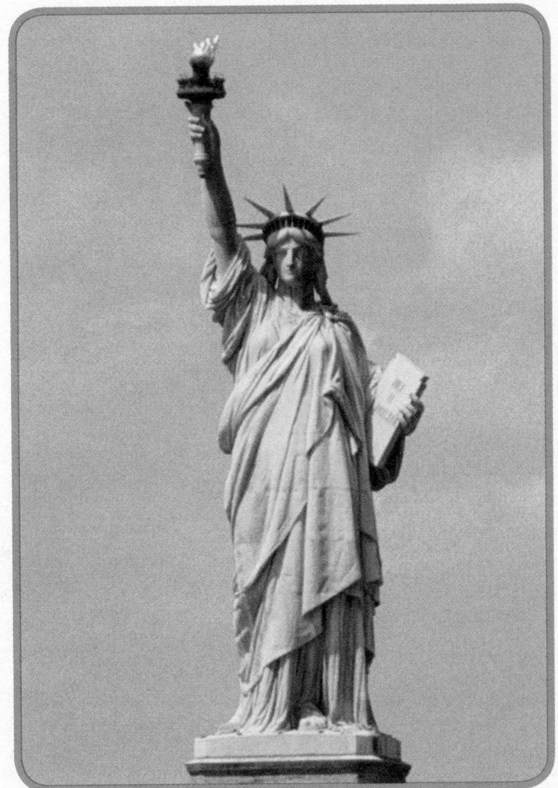

Teaching Note: Explain that a symbol is something that stands for something else. Discuss how the symbols pictured stand for the United States and for freedom. Explain that *freedom* means people have rights. They have choices about where they live, work, play, and go to school. Discuss why freedom is an important belief.

Go online to access your interactive digital lesson.

Texas

Lesson 8

What are our country's symbols?

Texas Essential Knowledge and Skills

10.A Identify the flags of the United States and Texas.
14.B Obtain information about a topic using a variety of valid visual sources such as pictures, symbols, electronic media, print material, and artifacts.
15.B Create and interpret visuals, including pictures and maps.

Check the symbols that stand for the United States.

Teaching Note: Read the prompt aloud. Point out the white box by each picture as the place to make a check mark. When children have completed the activity, discuss how the U.S. symbols contribute to our sense of belonging and what we believe in. Then have children tell which U.S. symbol they like most, and why.

Chapter 1

TEKS Practice

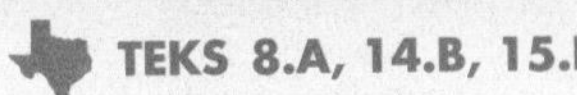

TEKS 8.A, 14.B, 15.B

1. **Circle** What rule do the children follow?

Please listen.

Raise your hand.

Work together.

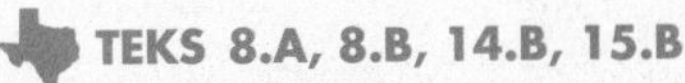

TEKS 8.A, 8.B, 14.B, 15.B

2. **Circle** Why do we follow this law?

to keep us happy

to keep us safe

to keep us busy

TEKS 8.B

3. **Match** Draw a line from the words to a matching picture.

home rule

school rule

community rule

Chapter 1

TEKS Practice

 TEKS 14.B, 15.B, 16.A

4. **Circle** What is the best way to solve this problem?

Turn and walk away.

One child swings.

Take turns and share.

 TEKS 10.D, 16.B

5. **Circle** Why do we vote?

to make a decision

to be helpful

to wait your turn

Chapter 1

TEKS Practice

TEKS 9.B

6. **Main Idea and Details**

Circle What is the main idea?

Leaders help us follow rules.
A parent helps us at home.
A teacher helps us at school.
A police officer helps us in the community.

TEKS 10.A, 14.B

7. **Circle** What does the United States flag stand for?

our community

our state

our country

TEKS 9.A

8. **Match** Draw a line from the words to a matching picture.

home leader

school leader

community leader

myStory Book

Draw people working together to do a job. 

Texas Essential Knowledge and Skills

15.B Create and interpret visuals, including pictures and maps.

ELA 13 Students use elements of the writing process (planning, drafting) to compose text.

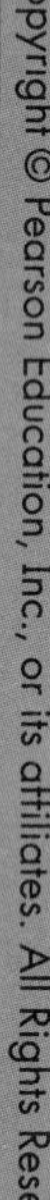

Teaching Note: Read the prompt aloud. Talk about different jobs that people do by working together. Help children identify a home, school, or community job that people might work together to do. Ask children to tell about their finished drawings.

PEARSON realize Go online to access your interactive digital lesson.

Texas

Chapter

2

Everybody Works

How do people get what they need?

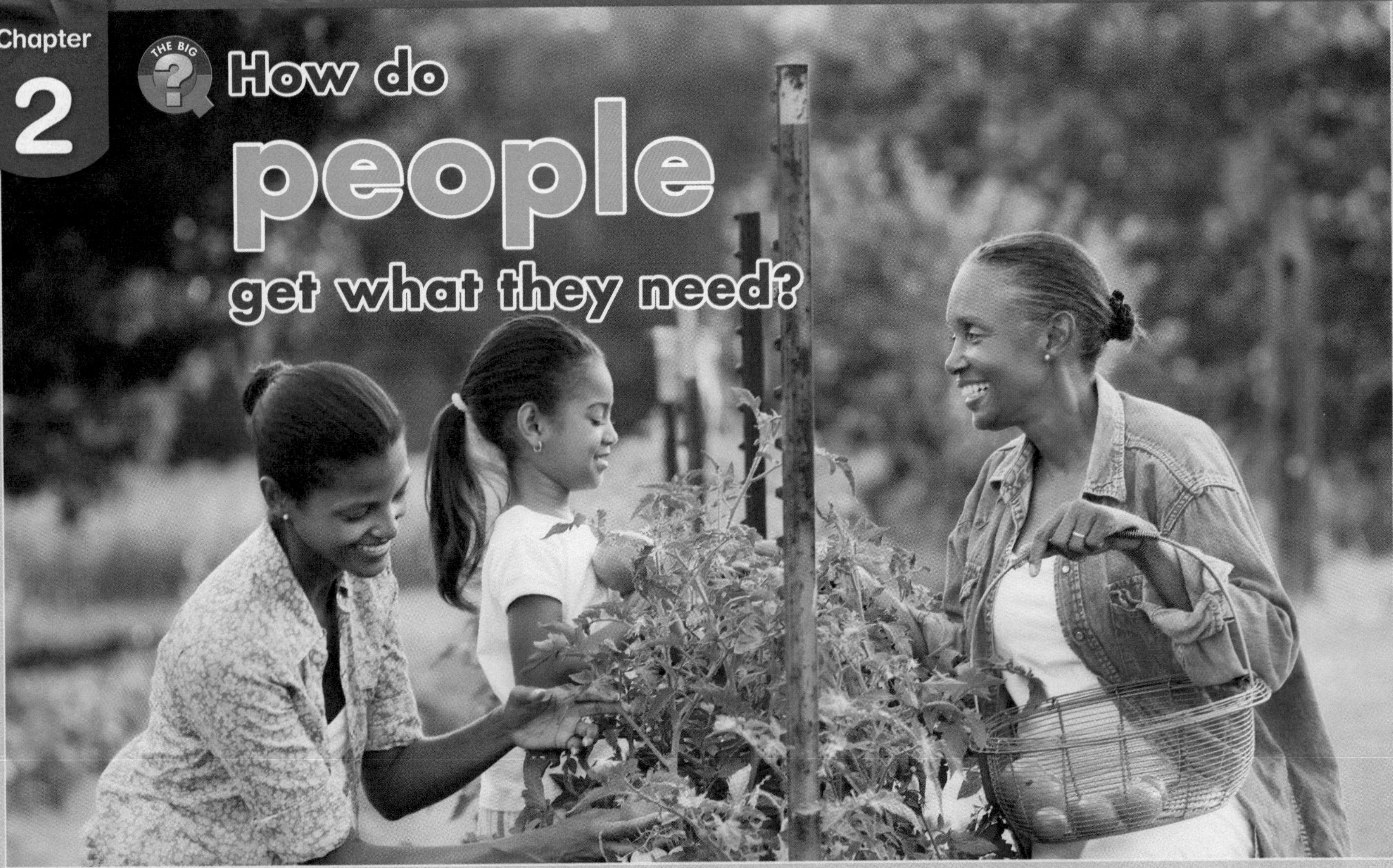

Teaching Note: Read the chapter title and the Big Question. Discuss what the people in the picture are doing. Ask: *What work are they doing? What do you think they will do with the tomatoes? Is food something that everybody needs? How do you know?*

Go online to access your interactive digital lesson.

Chapter 2

Everybody Works

Texas Essential Knowledge and Skills

15.B Create and interpret visuals, including pictures and maps.

my Story Spark

Draw a picture of a job you do at home.

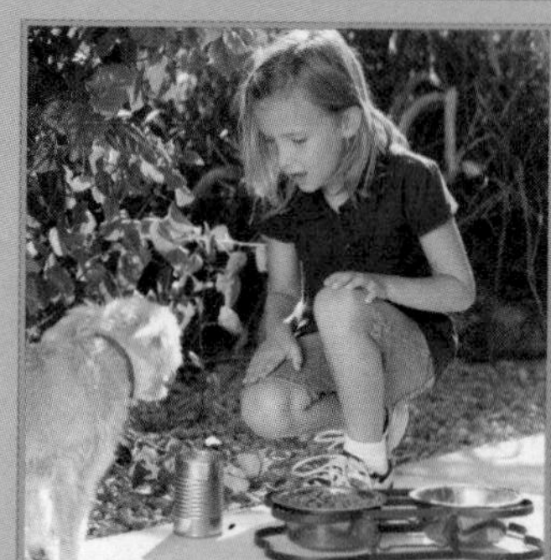

Teaching Note: Read the prompt aloud. Brainstorm jobs children do at home. Ask children to tell you what job they like to do or would like to do at home. Have children describe their finished drawings.

Chapter 2

Begin With a Song

Texas Essential Knowledge and Skills

7.A Identify jobs in the home, school, and community.

14.A Obtain information about a topic using a variety of valid oral sources such as conversations, interviews, and music.

15.B Create and interpret visuals, including pictures and maps.

Lots of Jobs

Sing to the tune of "Skip to My Lou."

Baker, teacher,
doctor, too.

Lots of jobs
I'd like to do.

Care for animals
in the zoo.

What kinds of work
would you do?

Teaching Note: Sing the song with children as you point to the pictures. Help children identify the tools used by a baker, a teacher, and a doctor; then identify the hats used by a cowboy, a firefighter, and a construction worker. Discuss what the zookeeper is doing. Then talk about other home, school, and community jobs.

Go online to access your interactive digital lesson.

Chapter 2

Vocabulary Preview

Circle examples of these words in the picture.

needs

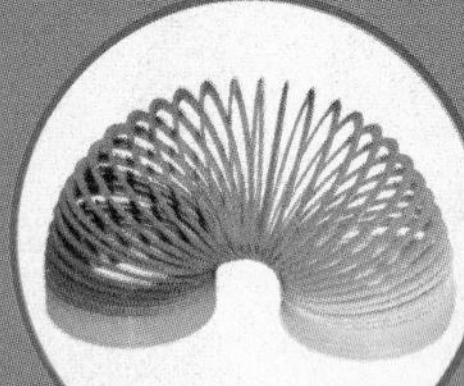

wants

money

job

goods

services

Fruit & Vegetable MARKETPLACE

Pat's Snacks

Teaching Note: Point to each photo and then read the word aloud. Use the photo to talk about what the word means. Ask children to describe what they see in the central picture. Then assist children in circling an example of each word in the picture.

What do we need? What do we want?

Texas Essential Knowledge and Skills

6.A Identify basic human needs of food, clothing, and shelter.
6.B Explain the difference between needs and wants.
15.A Express ideas orally based on knowledge and experiences.
15.B Create and interpret visuals, including pictures and maps.

Needs are things we must have to live.
Wants are things we like to have.

needs

wants

Teaching Note: Read the text. Identify *needs* as things people must have to live, such as food, clothing, and shelter. Identify *wants* as things people like but do not need. Help children distinguish needs from wants. Then brainstorm a list of basic human needs and wants. Discuss the difference between the items.

What do we need? What do we want?

Texas Essential Knowledge and Skills

6.A Identify basic human needs of food, clothing, and shelter.
6.B Explain the difference between needs and wants.
15.A Express ideas orally based on knowledge and experiences.
15.B Create and interpret visuals, including pictures and maps.

Draw lines to match each word with a picture. **Tell** why each thing is a need or a want.

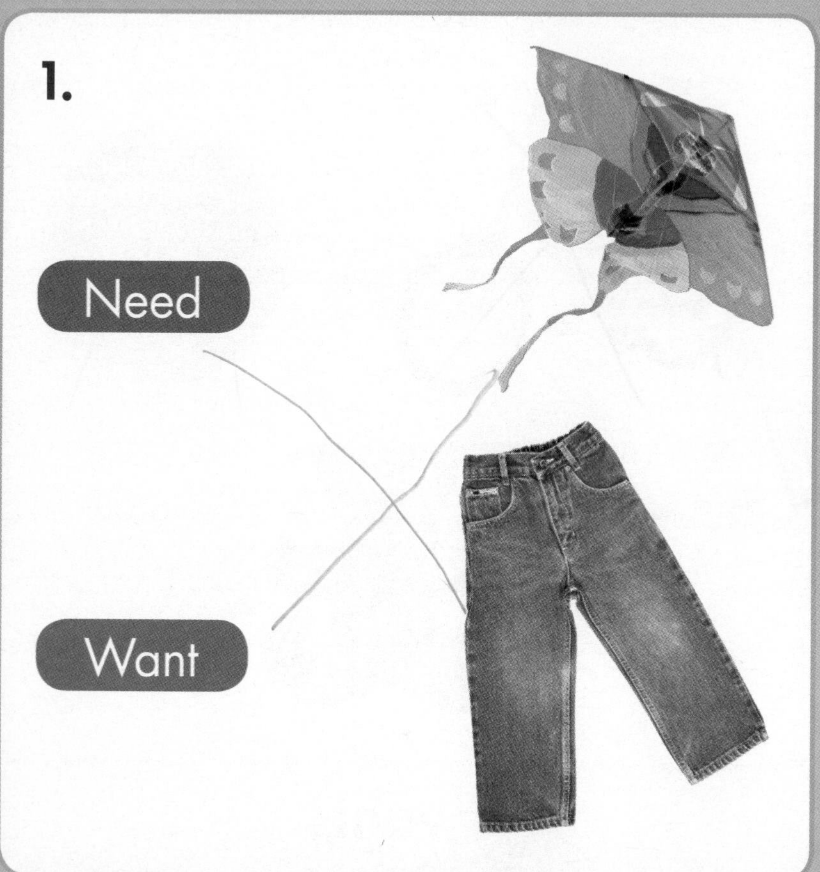

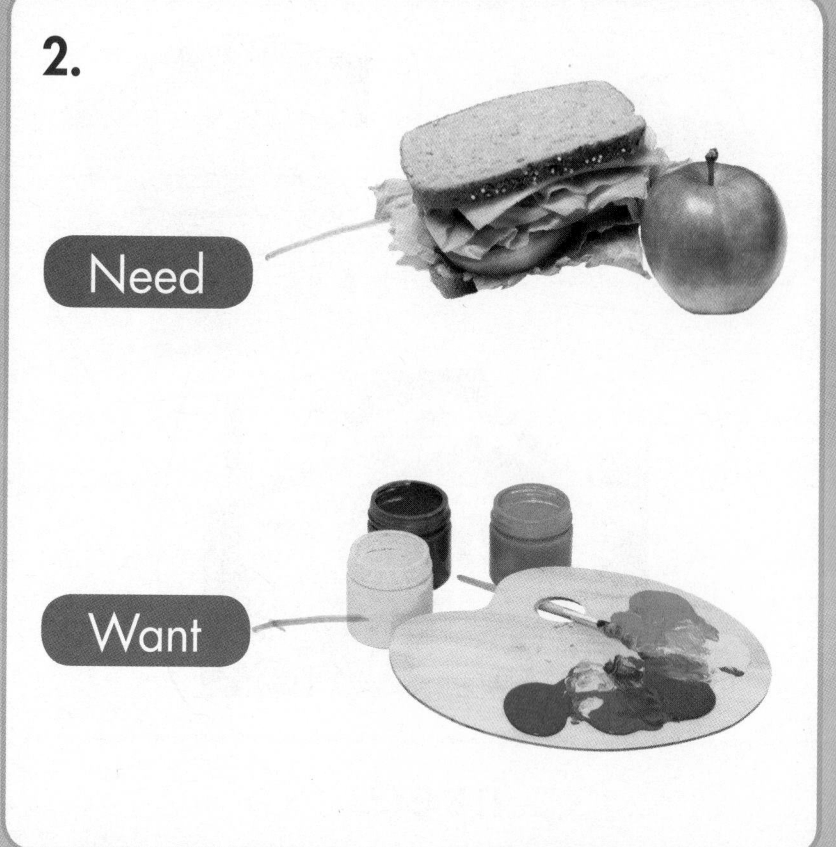

Teaching Note: Have children identify each photo and make a distinction between a basic human need and a want. Ask: *What picture shows something you need to live? What picture shows something you want but do not need to live?* Ask children to tell why they chose each answer. Have them identify what need is missing and why people need it.

How do we get what we need or want?

Texas Essential Knowledge and Skills

6.C Explain how basic human needs can be met such as through self-producing, purchasing, and trading.

14.B Obtain information about a topic using a variety of valid visual sources such as pictures, symbols, electronic media, print material, and artifacts.

15.B Create and interpret visuals, including pictures and maps.

We can trade.
We can make or grow things.
We can buy and sell.

Teaching Note: Discuss how people get what they need or want. Ask children if they have traded things with a friend. Discuss using money as a trade to buy things or sell things. Talk about how people grow or make things. Point to the picture on the right. Explain that the girl grew lemons to make and sell lemonade.

Go online to access your interactive digital lesson.

Texas

Lesson 2

How do we get what we need or want?

Texas Essential Knowledge and Skills

6.C Explain how basic human needs can be met such as through self-producing, purchasing, and trading.

14.B Obtain information about a topic using a variety of valid visual sources such as pictures, symbols, electronic media, print material, and artifacts.

15.B Create and interpret visuals, including pictures and maps.

Finish the drawing.
Show how they trade or sell.
Or, **show** how they make or grow things.

Teaching Note: Read the prompt aloud, and brainstorm examples of things that the children might grow, make, sell, or trade that would fit in the picture. Then have children complete the activity. Talk about the finished pictures.

Texas

Lesson 3

How do we earn money?

Texas Essential Knowledge and Skills

7.B Explain why people have jobs.

14.B Obtain information about a topic using a variety of valid visual sources such as pictures, symbols, electronic media, print material, and artifacts.

15.B Create and interpret visuals, including pictures and maps.

Some people do jobs to make money.
They buy things they need and want.

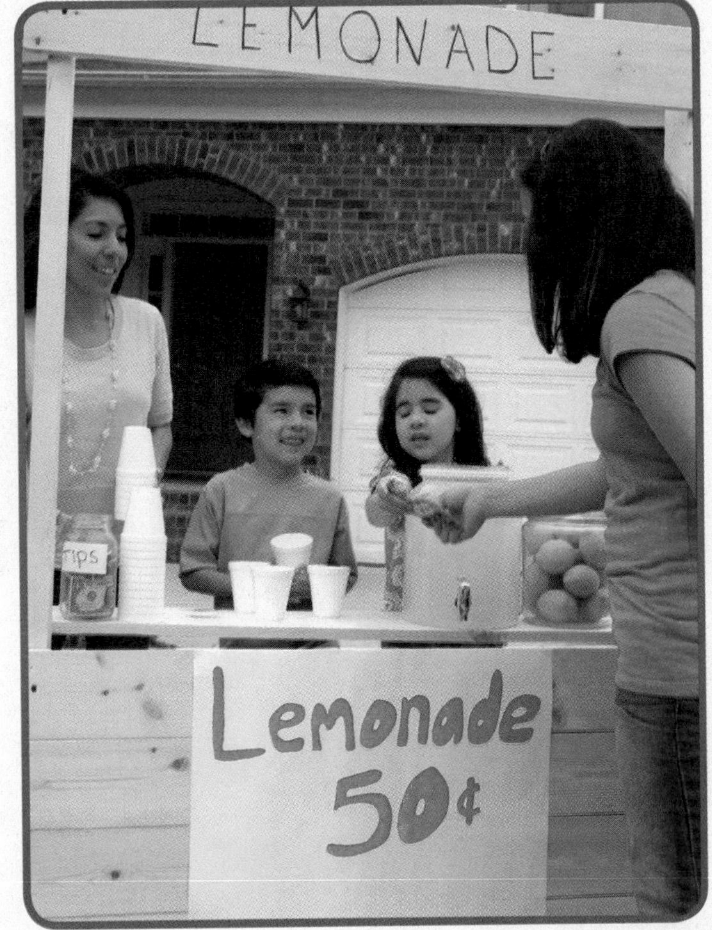

Teaching Note: Help children identify the dollar bill and each coin. Then discuss the picture on the right. Explain that a job is work people do to earn money in order to buy something they need or want. Talk about how one person gets a good he or she wants while another person earns money by selling the good.

Go online to access your interactive digital lesson.

How do we earn money?

Texas Essential Knowledge and Skills

7.B Explain why people have jobs.

14.B Obtain information about a topic using a variety of valid visual sources such as pictures, symbols, electronic media, print material, and artifacts.

15.B Create and interpret visuals, including pictures and maps.

Tell about a job you can do to make money.
Circle what you can buy with money.

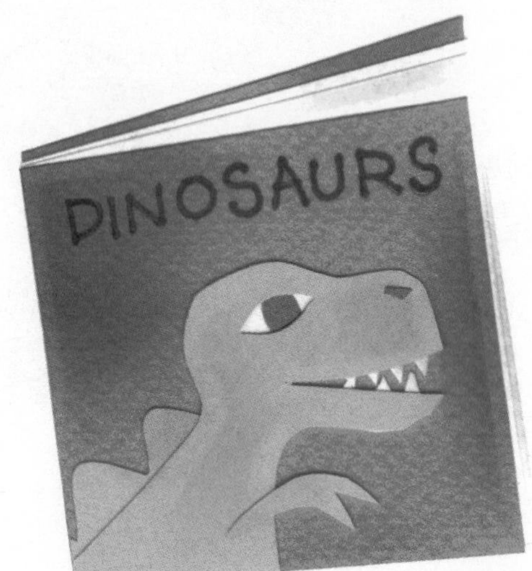

Teaching Note: Read the prompt aloud. Brainstorm and discuss jobs children might do to earn money, such as raking leaves or selling lemonade. Then talk about what each picture shows, and have children complete the activity. Discuss how money can be used to buy clothing and a book but not the sun or a mountain.

Reading Skills: Cause and Effect

TEKS

SS 7.B Explain why people have jobs.
SS 15.B Interpret visuals, including pictures.
ELA 4.A Predict what might happen next in text based on the illustrations.
ELA 10.C Discuss the ways authors group information in text.

A cause is what makes something happen.
An effect is what happens.

cause

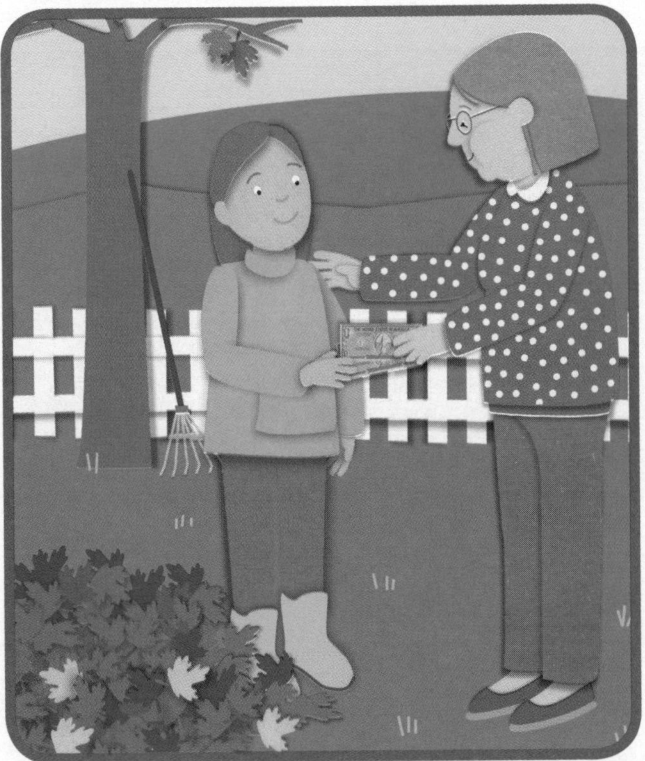

effect

Teaching Note: Help children learn *cause* and *effect* by using examples from the school day. Then discuss what the pictures show. Ask what job the girl was paid to do. Explain that earning money was the effect of raking leaves and that the girl's job caused her to earn money.

PEARSON realize Go online to access your interactive digital lesson.

Reading Skills: Cause and Effect

TEKS

SS 15.B Interpret visuals, including pictures.

ELA 4.A Predict what might happen next in text based on the illustrations.

ELA 10.C Discuss the ways authors group information in text.

Try it!

Look at the pictures. **Write C** on the cause. **Write E** on the effect.

Teaching Note: Read the prompts aloud. Discuss what each picture shows. Ask: *What is the effect of the cat pushing the vase? What caused the vase of flowers to fall to the floor and break?* Assist children in writing "C" and "E" on the correct picture.

Texas

Lesson 4

What are jobs that people do?

Texas Essential Knowledge and Skills

7.A Identify jobs in the home, school, and community.
7.B Explain why people have jobs.
14.B Obtain information about a topic using a variety of valid visual sources such as pictures, symbols, electronic media, print material, and artifacts.
15.B Create and interpret visuals, including pictures and maps.

People do many kinds of jobs.
Some people have jobs to make money.

home

school

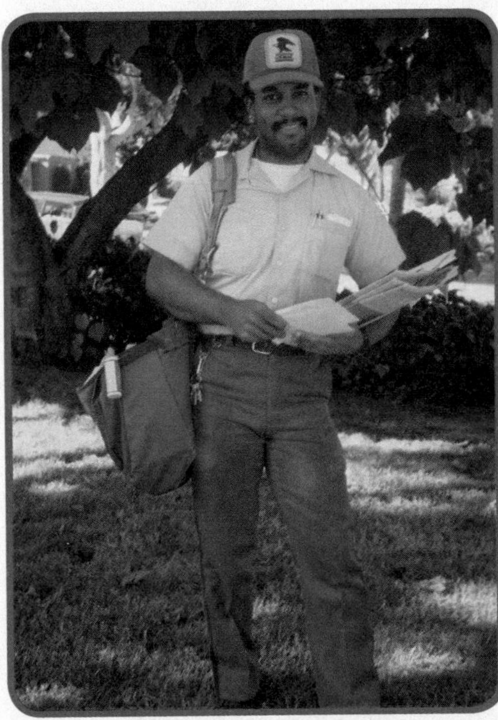

community

Teaching Note: Remind children that a job is work that a person may do to earn, or make, money. Explain that some people also do unpaid jobs as volunteers to help others. Discuss the jobs in the pictures. Talk about the different jobs people do at home, in your school, and in your community. Ask children about their favorite jobs at home.

Texas

Lesson 4

What are jobs that people do?

Texas Essential Knowledge and Skills

7.A Identify jobs in the home, school, and community.
7.B Explain why people have jobs.
14.B Obtain information about a topic using a variety of valid visual sources such as pictures, symbols, electronic media, print material, and artifacts.
15.B Create and interpret visuals, including pictures and maps.

Draw lines to match the workers with their tools.

Teaching Note: Read the prompt aloud. Help children identify each worker on the page and the tool the worker would need to do his or her job. Talk about what the workers do with their tools. Then brainstorm other jobs and the tools people use to do their work in the home, in the school, and in the community.

21C Collaboration and Creativity: Listening and Speaking

TEKS

SS 14.A Obtain information about a topic using valid oral sources such as interviews.

SS 15.A Express ideas orally based on knowledge and experiences.

ELA 21.A Listen attentively by facing speakers and asking questions.

ELA 22 Share information and ideas by speaking audibly and clearly.

Look and **listen** when a friend speaks.
Talk clearly when you speak.

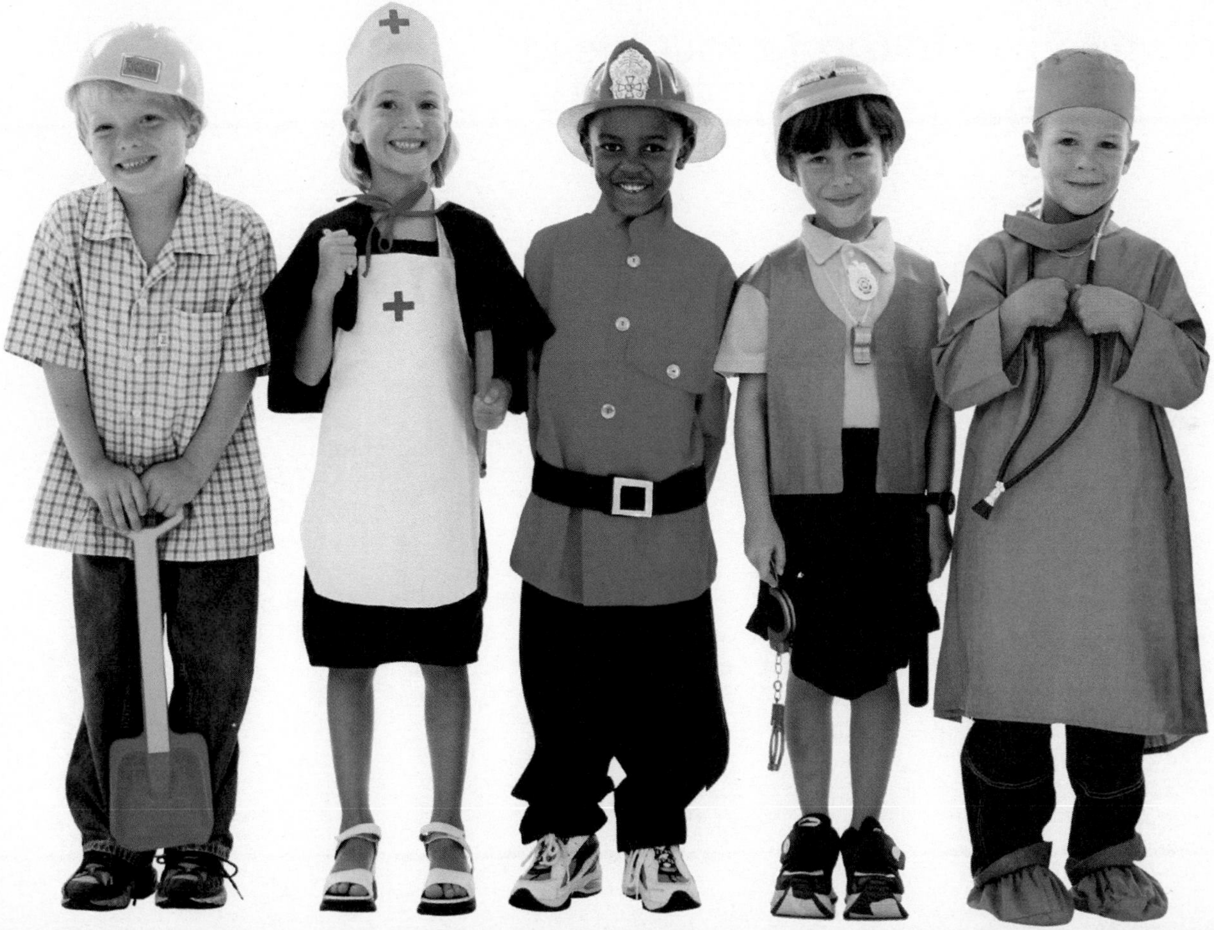

Teaching Note: Read the text aloud. Practice listening and speaking by talking with children about the job each child in the photo portrays. Model an interview to obtain information. Ask children which job they would like to do someday and why.

Go online to access your interactive digital lesson.

Collaboration and Creativity: Listening and Speaking

TEKS

SS 15.A Express ideas orally based on knowledge and experiences.

ELA 21.A Listen attentively by facing speakers and asking questions.

ELA 22 Share information and ideas by speaking audibly and clearly.

Try it!

Draw something you would like to buy.
Tell a friend why. Then **listen** to your friend.

Teaching Note: Read the prompts aloud. Have children complete their drawings. Then have children work with a partner to complete the second part of the activity. Be sure each child gets a turn to speak and a turn to listen.

Texas

Lesson 5

How do we use technology to meet our needs?

Texas Essential Knowledge and Skills

13.A Identify examples of technology used in the home and school.

13.B Describe how technology helps accomplish specific tasks and meet people's needs.

13.C Describe how his or her life might be different without modern technology.

14.B Obtain information about a topic using a variety of valid visual sources such as pictures, symbols, electronic media, print material, and artifacts.

15.B Create and interpret visuals, including pictures and maps.

We use tools and machines.
They help us do things faster.
They meet our needs, too.

Teaching Note: Point to each kind of technology, and ask children to identify it. Explain that these machines and tools help us meet our needs or help us accomplish different tasks more quickly. Describe what each tool or machine does. Discuss what people's lives would be like if we did not have each one. Brainstorm where we use each item.

Go online to access your interactive digital lesson.

How do we use technology to meet our needs?

Texas Essential Knowledge and Skills

13.A Identify examples of technology used in the home and school.

13.B Describe how technology helps accomplish specific tasks and meet people's needs.

13.C Describe how his or her life might be different without modern technology.

14.B Obtain information about a topic using a variety of valid visual sources such as pictures, symbols, electronic media, print material, and artifacts.

15.B Create and interpret visuals, including pictures and maps.

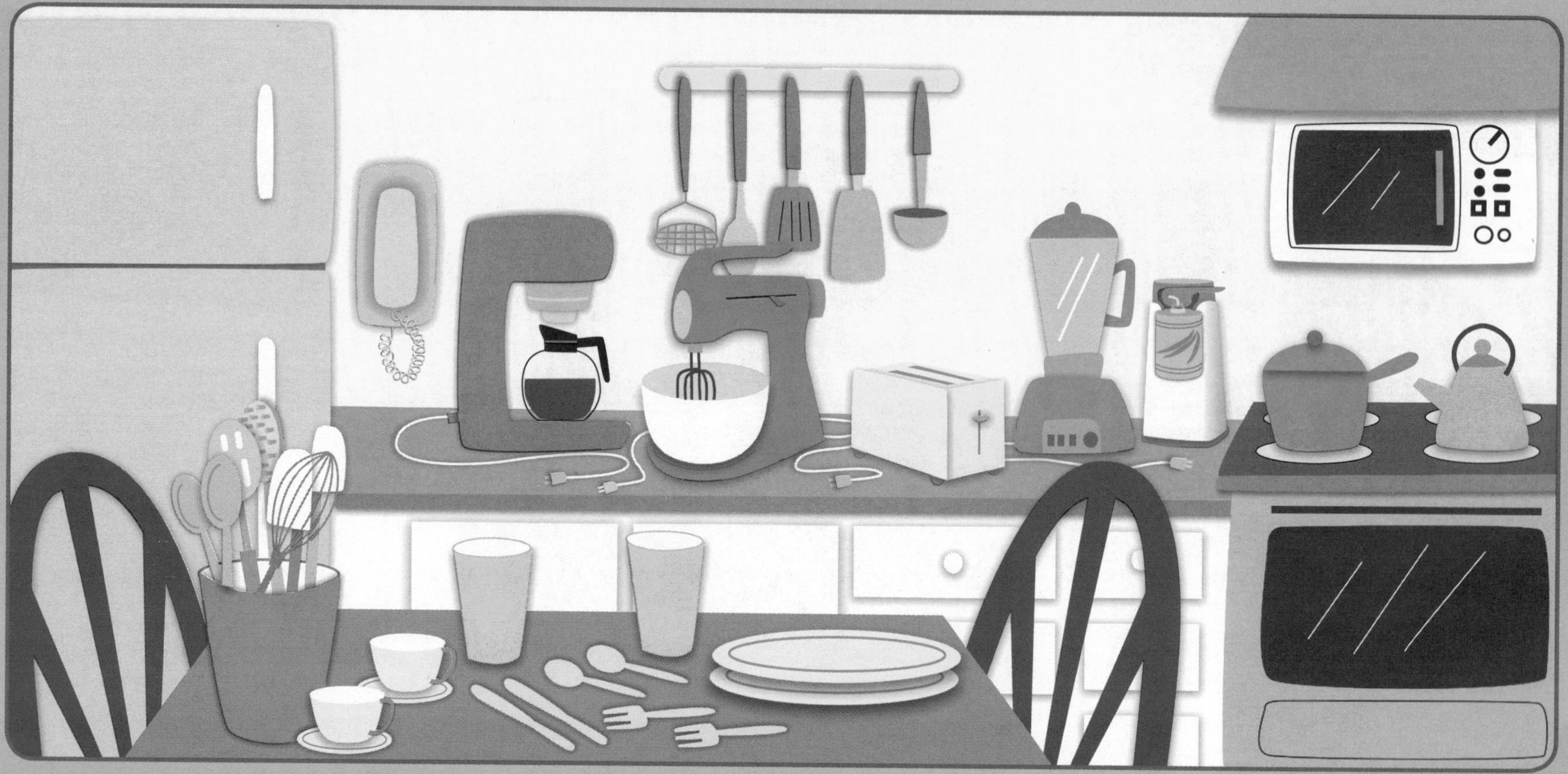

Circle tools and machines.
Tell what each one does and how it helps us.

Teaching Note: Read the prompt aloud. Discuss what the picture shows. Help children identify tools and machines that help them accomplish a task and meet their needs. Then have children complete the activity. Talk about what our lives would be like if we did not have each tool or machine.

Texas

Lesson 6

What are goods and services?

Texas Essential Knowledge and Skills

14.B Obtain information about a topic using a variety of valid visual sources such as pictures, symbols, electronic media, print material, and artifacts.

15.B Create and interpret visuals, including pictures and maps.

Goods are things people grow or make.
Services are work people do to help others.

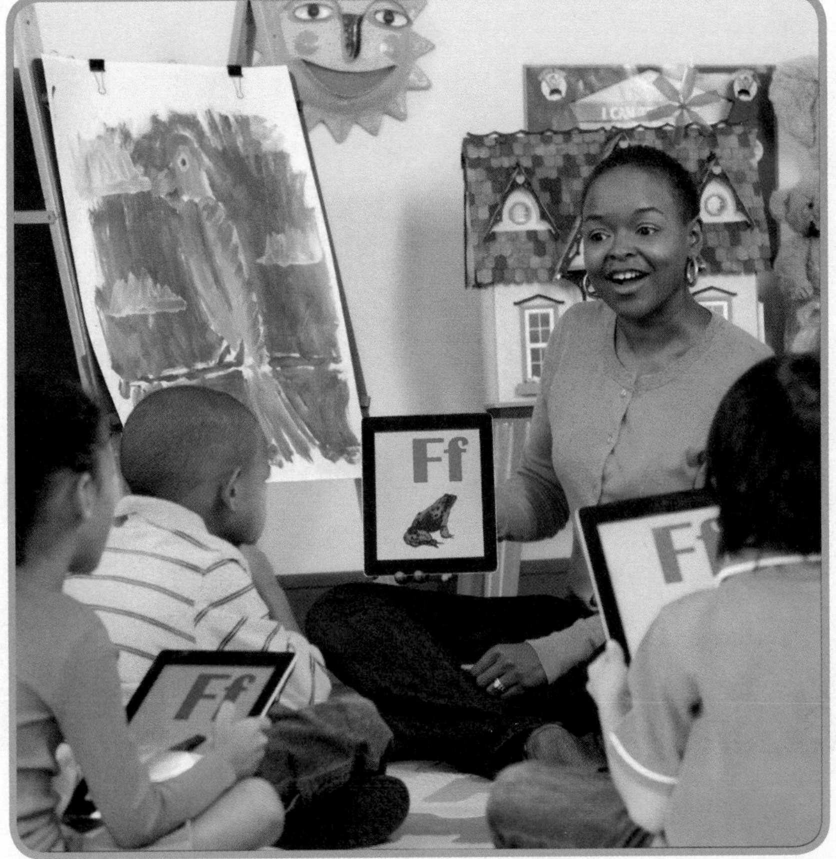

Teaching Note: Read the text aloud. Help children identify the goods in the photo on the left and the service in the photo on the right. Discuss other goods people grow or make, using classroom or home examples. Then talk about different service jobs in your community.

Go online to access your interactive digital lesson.

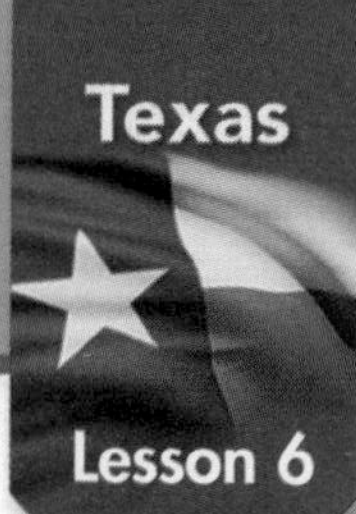

What are goods and services?

Texas Essential Knowledge and Skills

14.B Obtain information about a topic using a variety of valid visual sources such as pictures, symbols, electronic media, print material, and artifacts.

15.B Create and interpret visuals, including pictures and maps.

Write G on pictures that show goods.
Write S on pictures that show services.

Teaching Note: Write the letters "G" and "S", and have children copy them on a sheet of paper. Then read the prompts aloud. Help children identify which photos show goods and which show services. Assist children in writing "G" or "S" on each photo.

Chapter 2

TEKS Practice

 TEKS 6.A, 6.B, 14.B, 15.B

1. **Circle** What is something that you need to live?

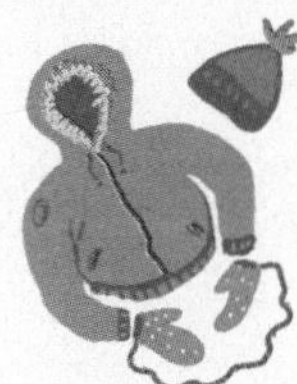

 TEKS 6.C, 14.B, 15.B

2. **Circle** What does this picture show?

We make and grow.
We buy and sell.
We trade.

 TEKS 6.A, 14.B, 15.B

3. **Match** Draw a line from the word to a matching picture that shows needs.

food

clothing

shelter

Chapter 2

TEKS Practice

TEKS 7.B

4. **Circle** Why do most people have jobs?

    to work hard
    to make money
    to meet people

TEKS 6.C, 7.B, 14.B, 15.B

5. **Cause and Effect**

    Circle Why is the girl selling lemonade?

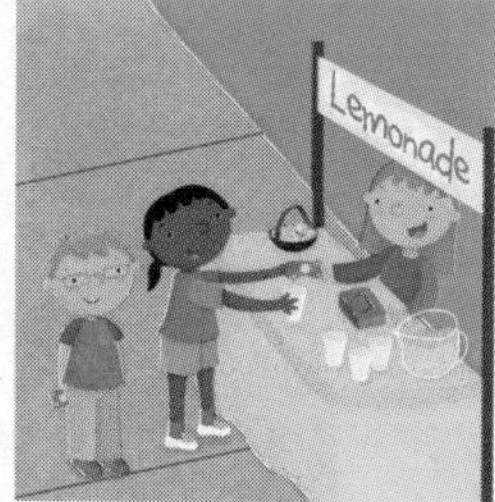

    to have fun
    to make money
    to make friends

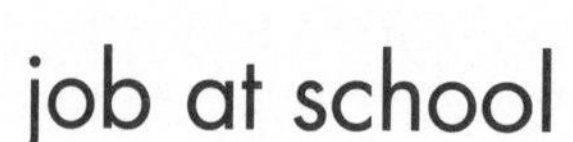

TEKS 7.A

6. **Match** Draw a line from the words to a matching picture.

job at home

job at school

job in the community

Chapter 2

TEKS Practice

 TEKS 13.B, 14.B, 15.B

7. **Circle** What is a machine that helps us do work?

 TEKS 13.C, 14.B, 15.B

8. **Circle** What would we do if we did not have telephones?

my Story Book

Texas Essential Knowledge and Skills

SS 15.B Create and interpret visuals, including pictures and maps.

ELA 13 Students use elements of the writing process (planning, drafting) to compose text.

Draw a picture of a job you would like.
Show what you would make or do for others. 

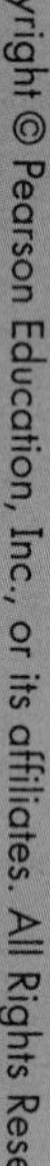

Teaching Note: Read the prompts aloud. Review and discuss the different types of jobs from the chapter. Then assist children as they complete the activity. When the drawing is finished, ask: *Does your picture show making, growing, or selling goods? Or does your picture show a service?*

PEARSON realize Go online to access your interactive digital lesson.

Where We Live

What is the world like?

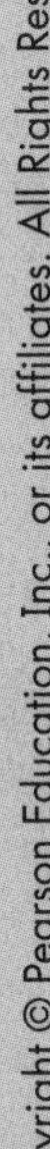

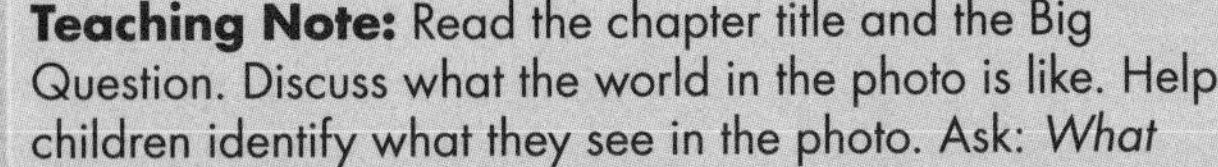

Teaching Note: Read the chapter title and the Big Question. Discuss what the world in the photo is like. Help children identify what they see in the photo. Ask: *What do you think the weather is like? Does it look hot or cold here? How do you know?*

Go online to access your interactive digital lesson.

Chapter 3

Where We Live

Texas Essential Knowledge and Skills

15.B Create and interpret visuals, including pictures and maps.

my Story Spark

Look out the window. **Draw** what you see.

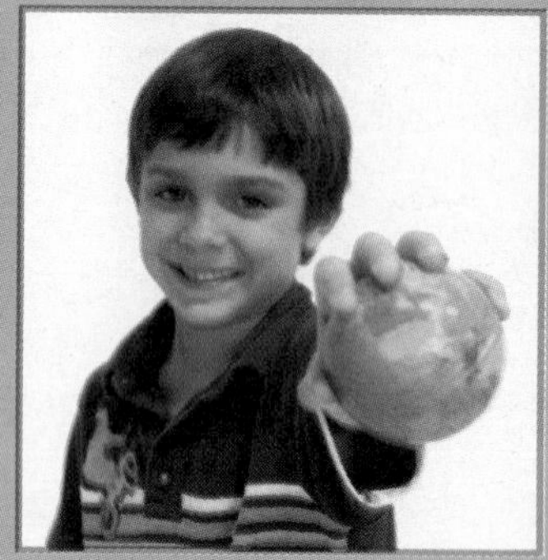

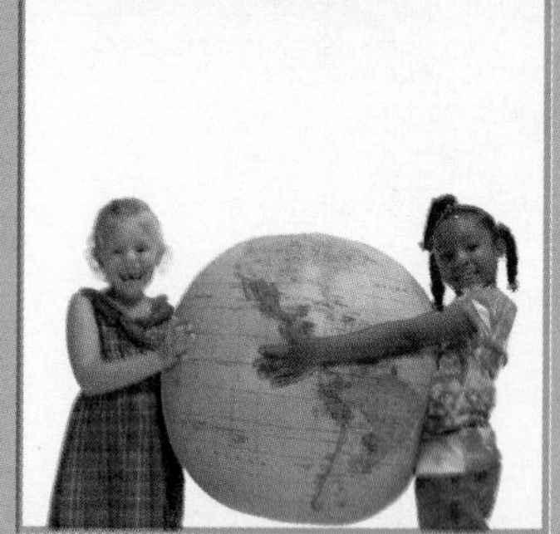

Teaching Note: Read the prompt aloud. Encourage children to look out a nearby window and focus on details in their drawing. Ask children to describe the drawing and show you from the window which object they chose to draw.

Begin With a Song

Texas Essential Knowledge and Skills

14.A Obtain information about a topic using a variety of valid oral sources such as conversations, interviews, and music.
15.B Create and interpret visuals, including pictures and maps.

This Is My Community

Sing to the tune of "Twinkle, Twinkle, Little Star."

This is where I live and play,
work and shop most every day.

Here's my home and here's my street.
This is where my neighbors meet.

Lots of people live near me.
This is my community!

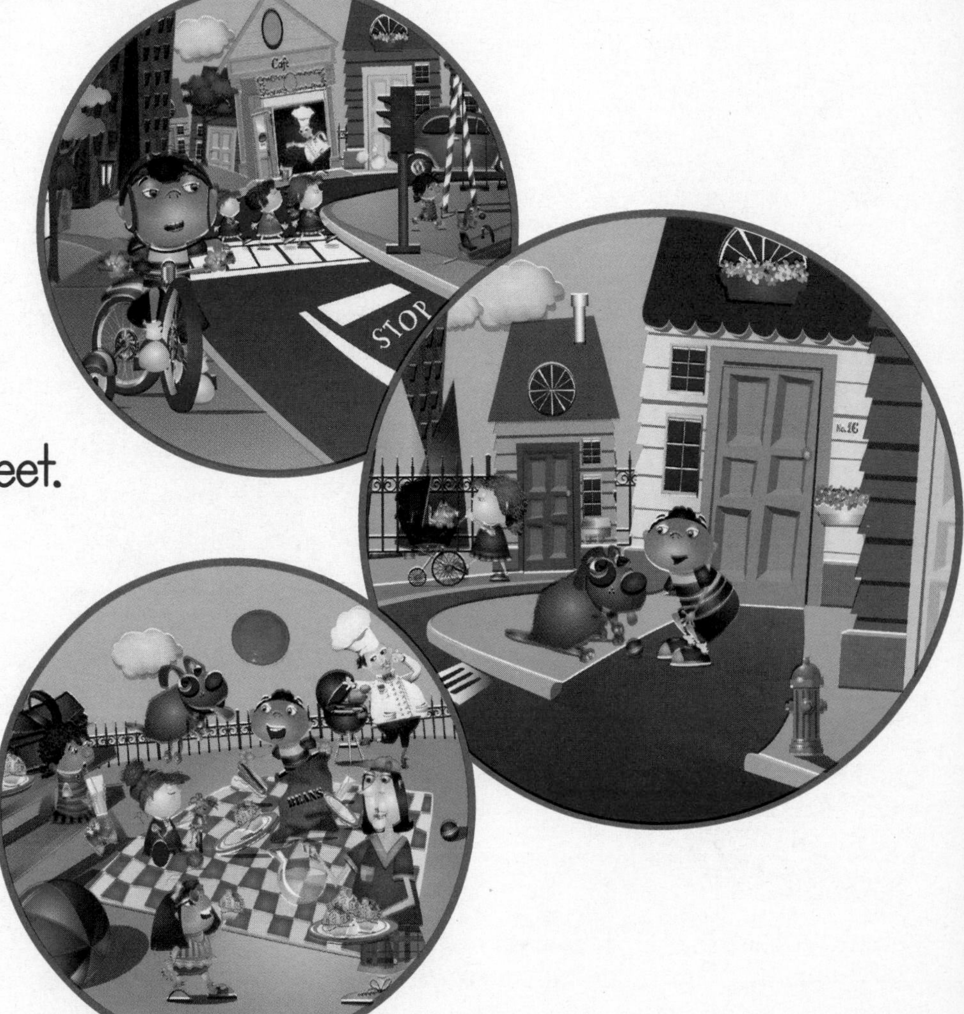

Teaching Note: Review the meaning of *community*. Then sing the song as you point to each picture. Invite children to sing with you. Discuss the features of your community and what children might see if they took a walk with you.

Go online to access your interactive digital lesson.

Chapter 3

Vocabulary Preview

Circle examples of these words in the picture.

map

hill

mountain

plain

river

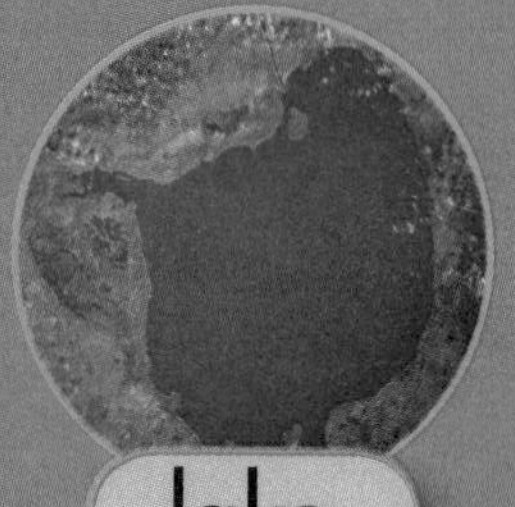

lake

Teaching Note: Read each word aloud as you point to the photo. Talk about the meaning of each word. Then ask children to describe what they see in the central picture. Assist them in circling an example of each word in the picture.

Where do we live?

Texas Essential Knowledge and Skills

4 Geography. The student understands the concept of location.
14.B Obtain information about a topic using a variety of valid visual sources such as pictures, symbols, electronic media, print material, and artifacts.
15.B Create and interpret visuals, including pictures and maps.

A neighborhood has many buildings.
Each building has an address.
An address tells the number and street name of a place.

Teaching Note: Define a neighborhood as the small area in which a person lives. Help children identify the neighborhood place in each picture. Then discuss places children may be familiar with in your school or home neighborhood.

Go online to access your interactive digital lesson.

Where do we live?

Texas Essential Knowledge and Skills

4 Geography. The student understands the concept of location.
14.B Obtain information about a topic using a variety of valid visual sources such as pictures, symbols, electronic media, print material, and artifacts.
15.B Create and interpret visuals, including pictures and maps.

Draw a picture of your home.
Tell your address.

Teaching Note: Read the prompt aloud. Have children draw a picture of their home. Then encourage children to recite their home address. If necessary, provide assistance.

Texas

Lesson 2

Where are places located?

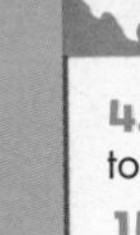

Texas Essential Knowledge and Skills

4.A Use terms, including over, under, near, far, left, and right, to describe relative location.

14.B Obtain information about a topic using a variety of valid visual sources such as pictures, symbols, electronic media, print material, and artifacts.

15.B Create and interpret visuals, including pictures and maps.

Some words tell us where places or things are located.

over

under

near

far

left

right

Teaching Note: Discuss the picture. Then read the location terms listed in the column on the right. Talk about the relative location of things in the picture using each term. For example: *The flower box is under the windows. The clock is over the school sign.* Use the terms *near, far, left,* and *right* to describe the location of other things.

PEARSON realize. Go online to access your interactive digital lesson.

Where are places located?

Texas Essential Knowledge and Skills

4.A Use terms, including over, under, near, far, left, and right, to describe relative location.

14.B Obtain information about a topic using a variety of valid visual sources such as pictures, symbols, electronic media, print material, and artifacts.

15.B Create and interpret visuals, including pictures and maps.

Think of two places in your neighborhood.
Draw them on the right and left of the library. **Label** each place.

library

Teaching Note: Discuss places in your school or neighborhood. Make a list for children to see. Read it aloud. Encourage children to use the list to draw two places. Ask children to describe the completed drawings. Then use the terms *over, under, left, near, far, left,* and *right* to discuss the location of things in the classroom.

Lesson 3

Maps show places and their locations. They can show big places or small places. They can show land and water.

Texas Essential Knowledge and Skills

4.A Use terms, including over, under, near, far, left ... to describe relative location.

... near, far, left, and right,

... tion, including

... variety of valid ... ic media, print material, and artifacts ...

15.B Create and interpret visuals, in... ures and maps.

Teaching Note: Explain that the large map shows a big place, our country, and the smaller map shows a small place, a neighborhood. Point out your state on the U.S. map. Then use location words to ask questions about each map, such as: *What states are near Louisiana? What is in front of the school?*

Go online to access your interactive digital lesson.

What do maps show?

and right,

4.C Identify tools that aid in determining location, including maps and globes.

14.B Obtain information about a topic using a variety of valid visual sources such as pictures, symbols, electronic media, print material, and artifacts.

15.B Create and interpret visuals, including pictures and maps.

Tell what the map shows.

Circle the teacher's desk on the map.

Draw a place where children can read books.

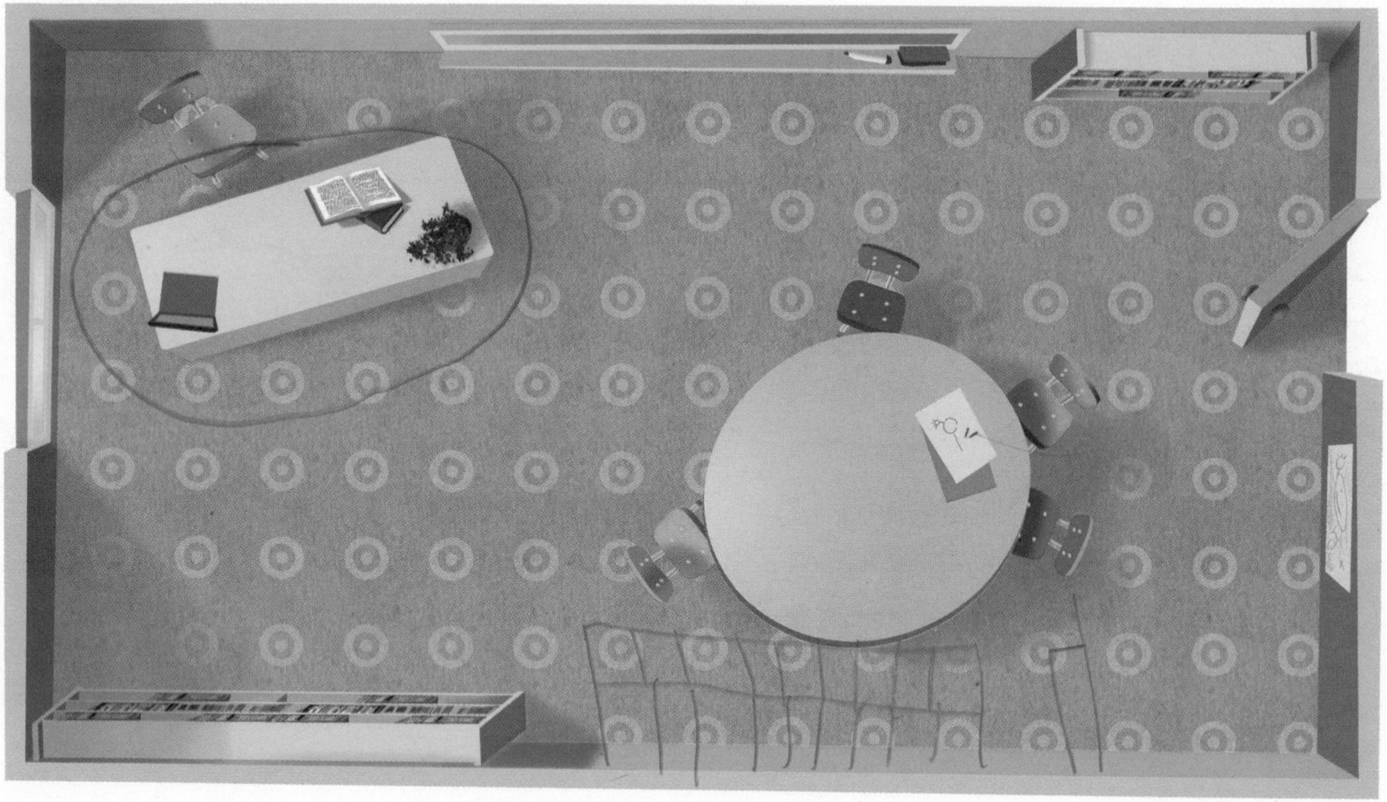

Teaching Note: Help children understand that the map shows a view of a classroom from above, and identify what is shown on the map. Then read the prompts aloud, and have children complete the activity. Have them use terms such as *near, far, over, under, left,* or *right* to describe the location of objects on the map.

21C Map Skills: Using a Map Key

TEKS

SS 4.B Locate places on the school campus and describe their relative locations.

SS 4.C Identify tools that aid in determining location, including maps.

SS 14.B Obtain information about a topic using visual sources.

SS 15.B Interpret visuals, including maps.

A map key tells you what the symbols on a map mean. Symbols stand for real things.

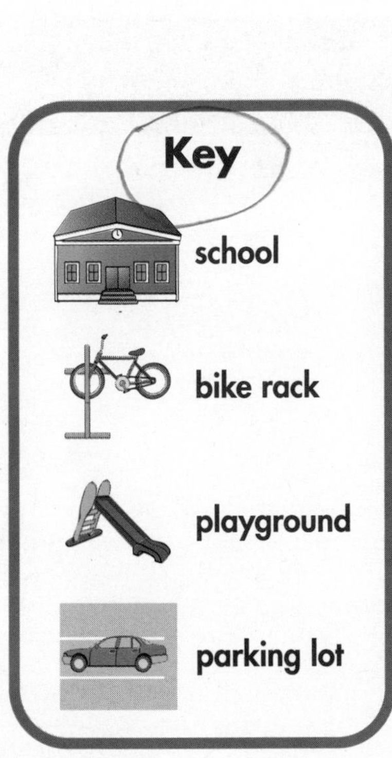

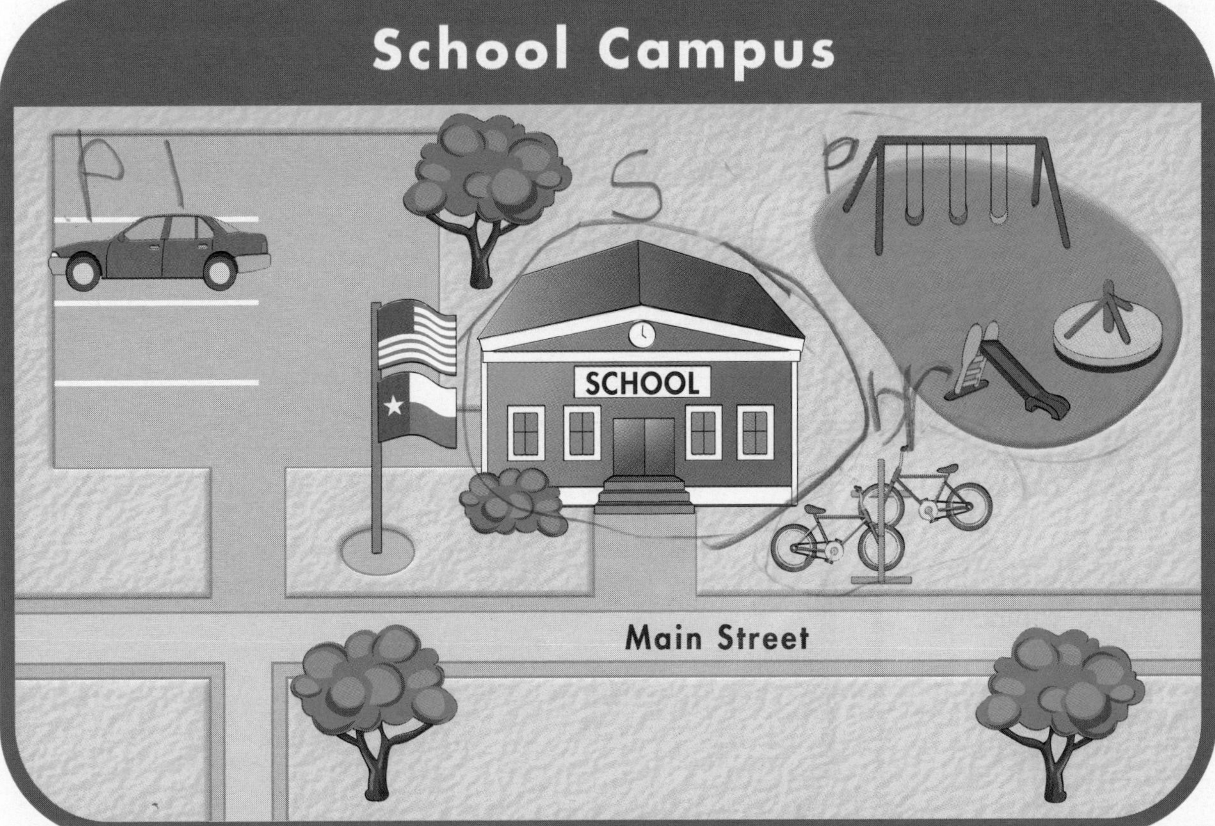

Teaching Note: Point to the symbol for the school in the key, and then point to the school on the map. Help children locate all the places on the map using the symbols in the key. Then ask questions so children can locate places on the school campus and describe their relative locations. Ask: *What place is located to the right of the school?*

PEARSON realize — Go online to access your interactive digital lesson.

Map Skills: Using a Map Key

TEKS

SS 4.B Locate places on the school campus and describe their relative locations.

SS 4.C Identify tools that aid in determining location, including maps.

SS 14.B Obtain information about a topic using visual sources.

SS 15.B Interpret visuals, including maps.

Name the symbols in the key. **Make** a map of your classroom. **Draw** the symbols on the map. **Tell** about your map.

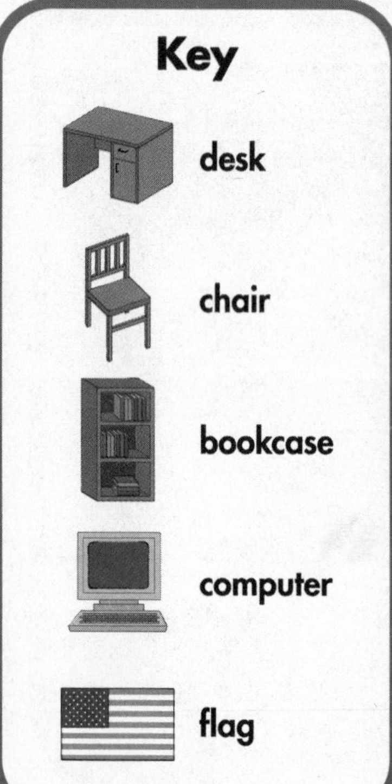

Teaching Note: Ask: *Where is our classroom located?* Remind children that the classroom is located inside a building on the school campus. Then help them name the symbols in the key. Discuss where the symbols should go on the classroom map. Have children complete the activity and then describe the relative location of each item on the map.

Texas

Lesson 4

What do globes show?

Texas Essential Knowledge and Skills

4.C Identify tools that aid in determining location, including maps and globes.

5.A Identify the physical characteristics of place such as landforms, bodies of water, natural resources, and weather.

14.B Obtain information about a topic using a variety of valid visual sources such as pictures, symbols, electronic media, print material, and artifacts.

15.B Create and interpret visuals, including pictures and maps.

A globe is a model of Earth.
It shows land and water.

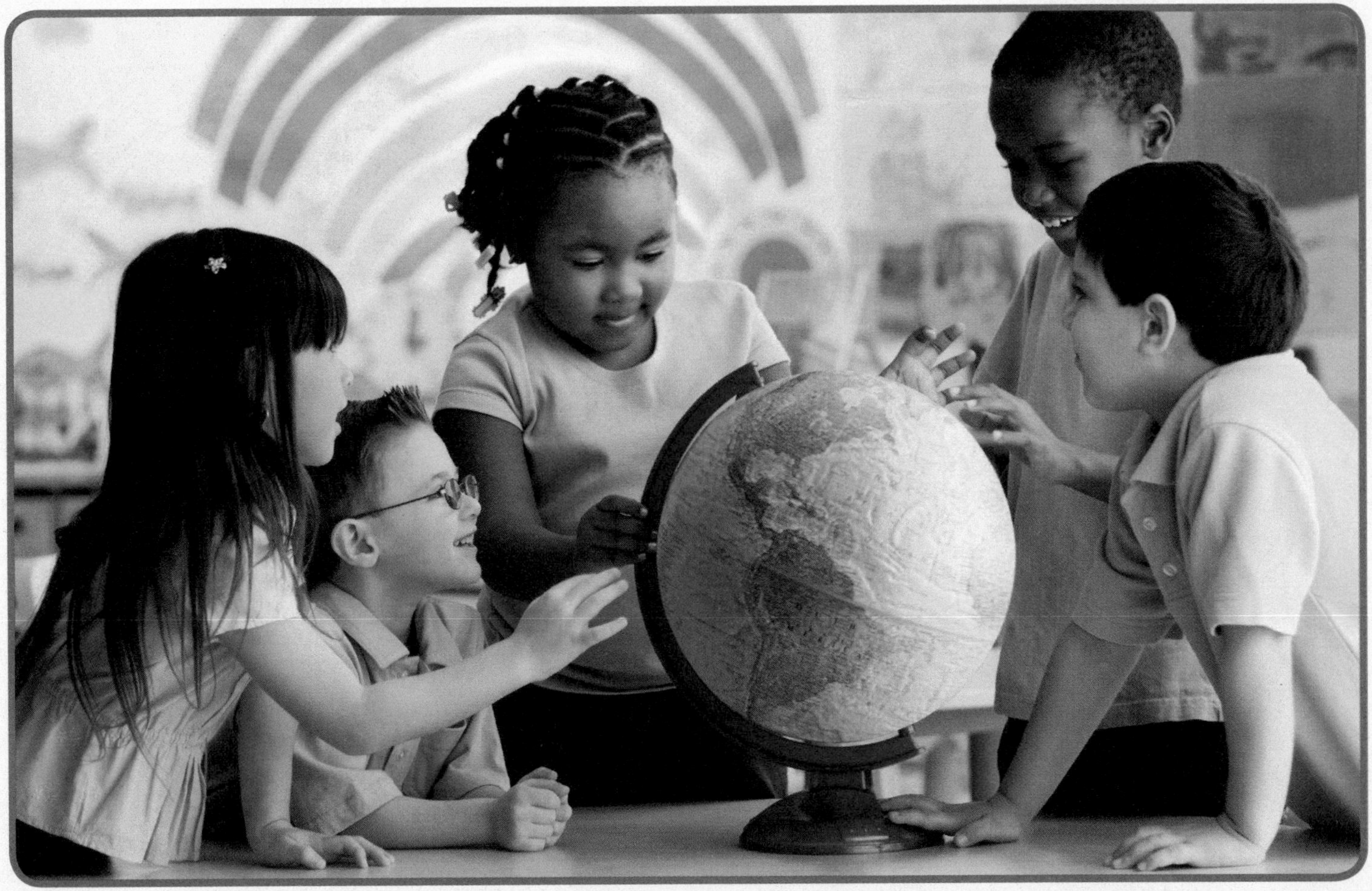

Teaching Note: If available, display a globe. Explain that it is a tool that helps us determine the location of places. Have children examine it. Ask: *How is a globe a model of Earth?* Discuss the globe's shape and what it shows. Explain what colors on the globe represent. Have children point to land and bodies of water on the globe.

Texas

Lesson 4

What do globes show?

Texas Essential Knowledge and Skills

4.C Identify tools that aid in determining location, including maps and globes.

5.A Identify the physical characteristics of place such as landforms, bodies of water, natural resources, and weather.

14.B Obtain information about a topic using a variety of valid visual sources such as pictures, symbols, electronic media, print material, and artifacts.

15.B Create and interpret visuals, including pictures and maps.

Color the water blue.
Color the land green.

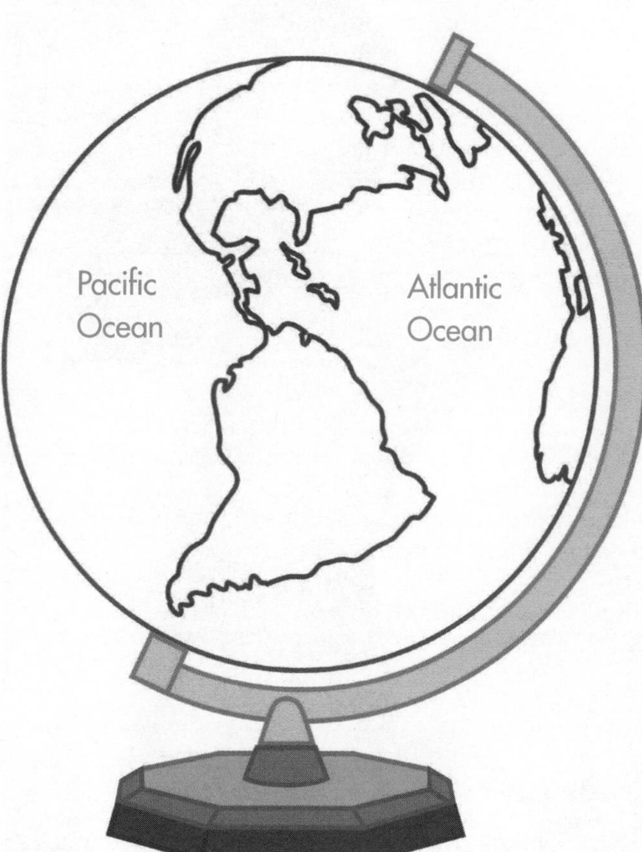

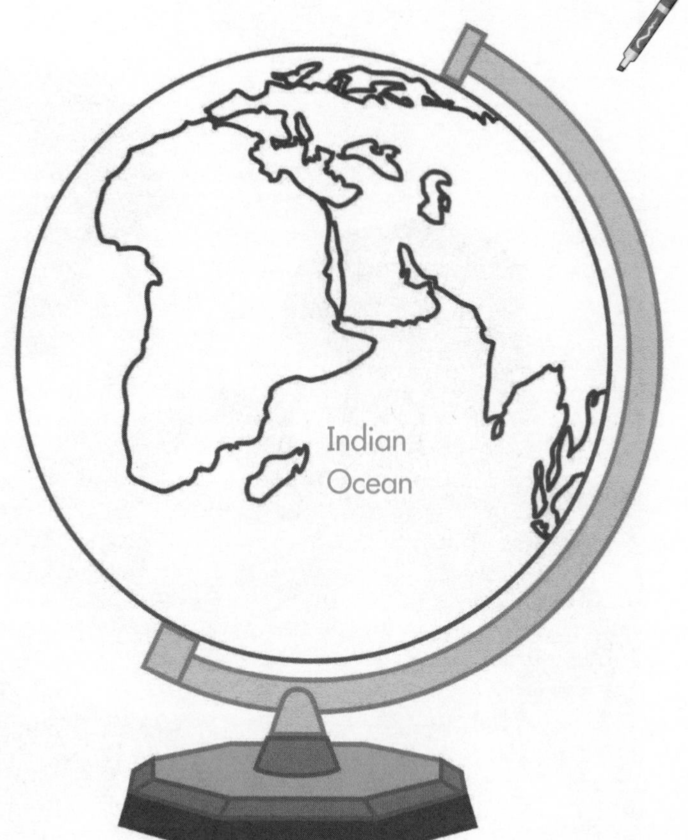

Teaching Note: Point to the illustrations. Explain that each globe shows a different side of the earth. Compare the illustrations with the photo on the previous page. Then provide a blue crayon and a green crayon, and have children color the land and bodies of water.

Texas

Lesson 5

What are landforms and bodies of water?

Texas Essential Knowledge and Skills

4.C Identify tools that aid in determining location, including maps and globes.

5.A Identify the physical characteristics of place such as landforms, bodies of water, natural resources, and weather.

14.B Obtain information about a topic using a variety of valid visual sources such as pictures, symbols, electronic media, print material, and artifacts.

15.B Create and interpret visuals, including pictures and maps.

There are different kinds of land.
There are different kinds of water.

Texas

Oklahoma
New Mexico
Arkansas
Louisiana
Cedar Creek Lake
Rio Grande
MEXICO
Gulf of Mexico

Key
mountains
river
plains
lake

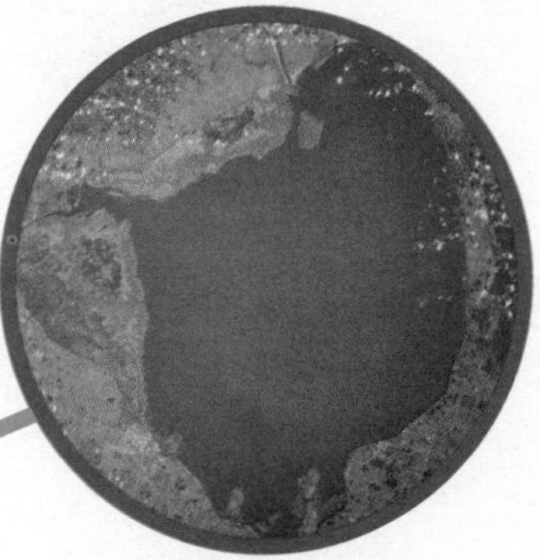

river

mountain

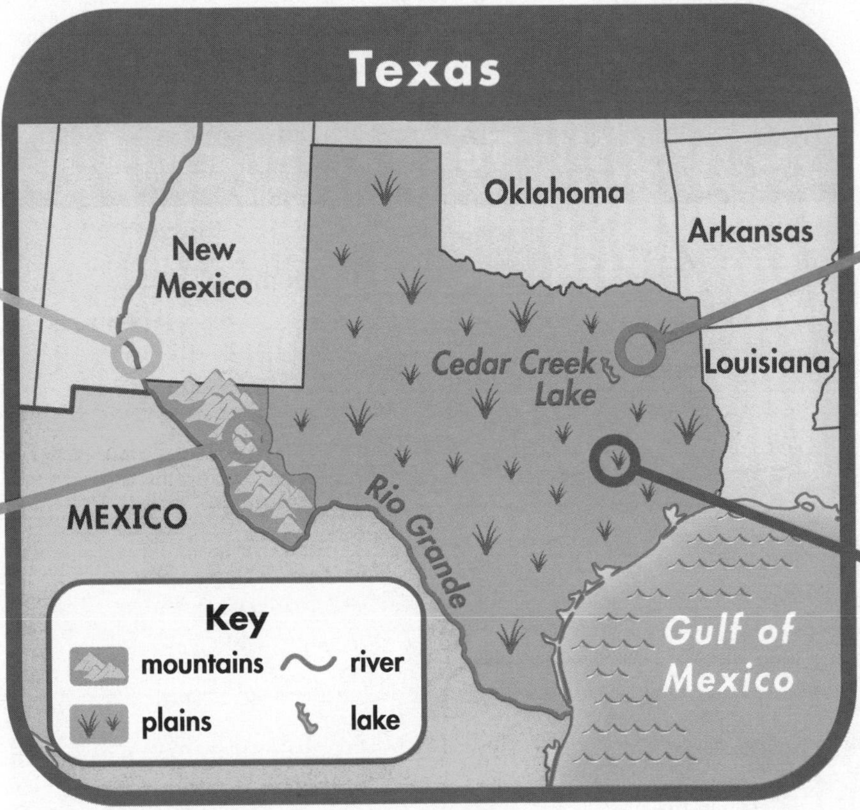

lake

plain

Teaching Note: Discuss the photos and the names of the landforms and bodies of water. Mention that Cedar Creek Lake is also called Cedar Creek Reservoir. Then have children use a finger to trace each line from a photo to the map. Talk about how the different kinds of land and water are pictured in symbols and colors on the map.

Go online to access your interactive digital lesson.

What are landforms and bodies of water?

Texas Essential Knowledge and Skills

4.C Identify tools that aid in determining location, including maps and globes.
5.A Identify the physical characteristics of place such as landforms, bodies of water, natural resources, and weather.
14.B Obtain information about a topic using a variety of valid visual sources such as pictures, symbols, electronic media, print material, and artifacts.
15.B Create and interpret visuals, including pictures and maps.

Look at the map.
Circle the mountains and plains.
Draw an X on the river and lake.

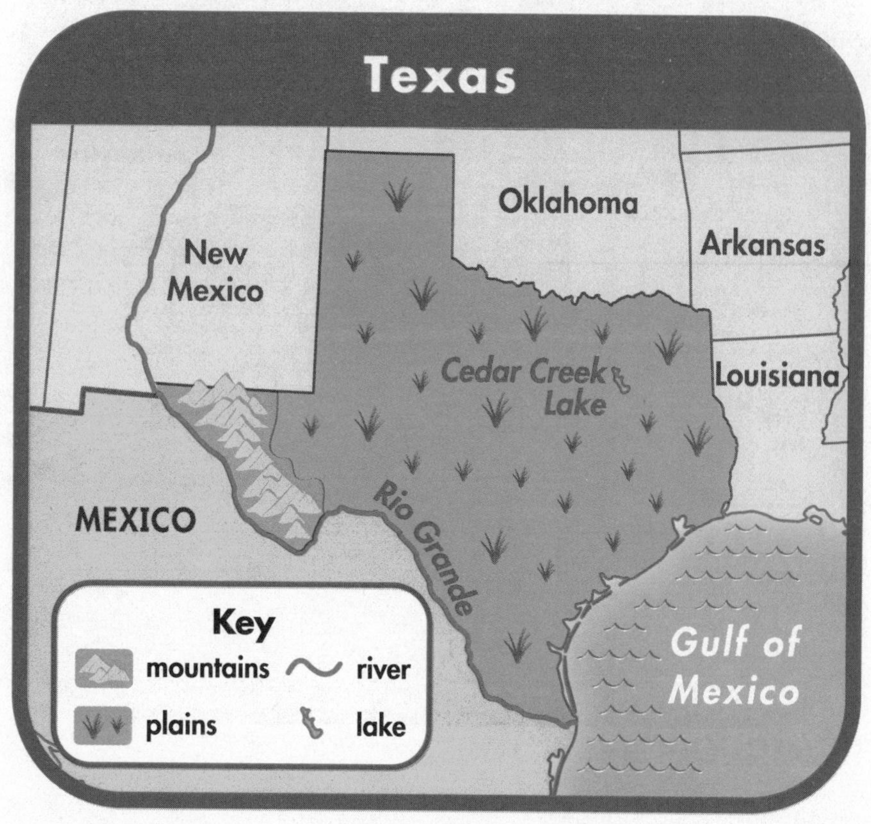

Teaching Note: Explain that the same map on the first page is shown here. Have children match the landform and water symbols in the directions and the key to those on the map. Then read the prompts aloud, and have children complete the activity.

Reading Skills: Classify and Categorize

TEKS

SS 5.A Identify the physical characteristics of place such as landforms and bodies of water.

ELA 5.C Identify and sort pictures of objects into categories.

You can put things into groups when they are like each other.

A hill and a mountain are landforms.

A river and an ocean are bodies of water.

Teaching Note: Review the names for different landforms and bodies of water children have learned. Explain that these terms can be grouped as *land* or *water*. Discuss the physical characteristics of land and water. Then talk about what is shown in each picture.

Reading Skills: Classify and Categorize

TEKS

SS 5.A Identify the physical characteristics of a place such as landforms and bodies of water.
ELA 5.C Identify and sort pictures of objects into categories.

Try it!

Circle in **brown** the pictures that show kinds of land.
Circle in **blue** the pictures that show kinds of water.

Teaching Note: Provide children with a blue crayon and a brown crayon. Discuss what is shown in each photo. Then read aloud the prompts, and have children complete the activity. Assist as needed.

Texas

Lesson 6

What is weather like?

Texas Essential Knowledge and Skills

5.A Identify the physical characteristics of place such as landforms, bodies of water, natural resources, and weather.

5.B Identify how the human characteristics of place such as ways of earning a living, shelter, clothing, food, and activities are based upon geographic location.

14.B Obtain information about a topic using a variety of valid visual sources such as pictures, symbols, electronic media, print material, and artifacts.

15.B Create and interpret visuals, including pictures and maps.

Weather is what the air is like outside.
Weather is not the same everywhere.
Weather can change, too.

rainy

cold

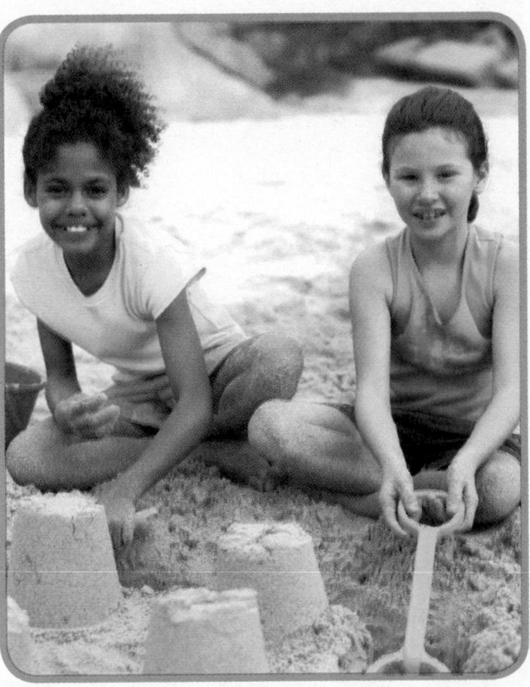

hot

Teaching Note: Explain what weather is. Talk about what the weather is like outside today and clothing we wear in this kind of weather. Ask children to describe each photo. Explain that weather in one place can be different from the weather in another place. Describe activities you can do in each geographic location.

PEARSON realize — Go online to access your interactive digital lesson.

Texas

Lesson 6

What is weather like?

Texas Essential Knowledge and Skills

5.A Identify the physical characteristics of place such as landforms, bodies of water, natural resources, and weather.

5.B Identify how the human characteristics of place such as ways of earning a living, shelter, clothing, food, and activities are based upon geographic location.

14.B Obtain information about a topic using a variety of valid visual sources such as pictures, symbols, electronic media, print material, and artifacts.

15.B Create and interpret visuals, including pictures and maps.

Look at each kind of weather.
Draw a line to what you would wear.

Teaching Note: Use weather words from the previous page to talk about each scene at the top. Discuss the clothing and weather items shown in each picture at the bottom. Ask: *What do people wear in hot (cold, rainy) weather?* Read the prompts, and have children complete the activity.

Texas

Lesson 7

What are the seasons?

> **Texas Essential Knowledge and Skills**
>
> **5.A** Identify the physical characteristics of place such as landforms, bodies of water, natural resources, and weather.
>
> **14.B** Obtain information about a topic using a variety of valid visual sources such as pictures, symbols, electronic media, print material, and artifacts.
>
> **15.B** Create and interpret visuals, including pictures and maps.

There are four seasons.

spring

summer

fall

winter

Teaching Note: Read the text aloud. Then name the season with children as you point to each picture. Discuss the weather shown in each picture. Focus on how the tree changes in each season. Explain that the seasons and seasonal changes such as weather can vary in different places. Ask: *What is your favorite season? Why?*

Go online to access your interactive digital lesson.

Texas

Lesson 7

What are the seasons?

Texas Essential Knowledge and Skills

5.A Identify the physical characteristics of place such as landforms, bodies of water, natural resources, and weather.

14.B Obtain information about a topic using a variety of valid visual sources such as pictures, symbols, electronic media, print material, and artifacts.

15.B Create and interpret visuals, including pictures and maps.

Choose a season.

Draw things on and around the tree that show your season.

Teaching Note: Read the prompts aloud. Discuss what each of the four seasons is like and what the tree might look like in each season. Have children complete the activity. Then have them describe their finished drawings by naming each item and how it relates to the season.

Texas

Lesson 8

How do we use Earth's resources?

Texas Essential Knowledge and Skills

5.A Identify the physical characteristics of place such as landforms, bodies of water, natural resources, and weather.

14.B Obtain information about a topic using a variety of valid visual sources such as pictures, symbols, electronic media, print material, and artifacts.

15.B Create and interpret visuals, including pictures and maps.

We use Earth's resources to meet our needs.

Teaching Note: Point to each photo at the top. Explain what natural resource is shown. Follow the arrow down to the photo below. Explain how the resource is used to meet a need. Brainstorm additional resources from Earth and how we use them to meet our needs. Explain that resources, such as corn, are found in different places.

Go online to access your interactive digital lesson.

Texas

Lesson 8

How do we use Earth's resources?

Texas Essential Knowledge and Skills

5.A Identify the physical characteristics of place such as landforms, bodies of water, natural resources, and weather.

14.B Obtain information about a topic using a variety of valid visual sources such as pictures, symbols, electronic media, print material, and artifacts.

15.B Create and interpret visuals, including pictures and maps.

Circle in green Earth's resources.

Circle in red things people use or make.

Teaching Note: Help children identify the natural resources and objects shown in each picture. Provide a green crayon and a red crayon, and have children complete the activity. Discuss the choices children made.

Texas

Lesson 9

What are other places like?

Texas Essential Knowledge and Skills

5.B Identify how the human characteristics of place such as ways of earning a living, shelter, clothing, food, and activities are based upon geographic location.

14.B Obtain information about a topic using a variety of valid visual sources such as pictures, symbols, electronic media, print material, and artifacts.

15.B Create and interpret visuals, including pictures and maps.

People have different homes, clothing, and food in different places.
People do different jobs and activities, too.

Teaching Note: Explain that ways of earning a living, homes, clothing, food, and activities can be different depending on geographic location. Point to each picture, and encourage children to talk about the characteristics of each place. Discuss other aspects of the way people live based on their geographic location.

Go online to access your interactive digital lesson.

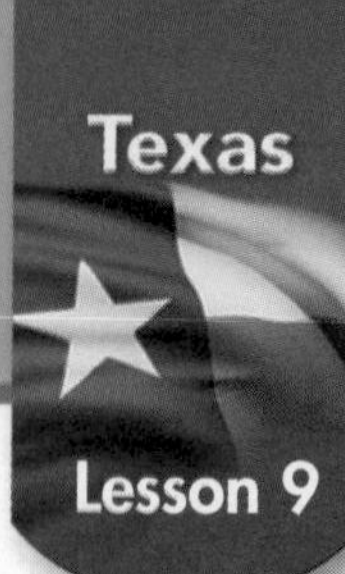

Texas

Lesson 9

What are other places like?

Texas Essential Knowledge and Skills

5.B Identify how the human characteristics of place such as ways of earning a living, shelter, clothing, food, and activities are based upon geographic location.

14.B Obtain information about a topic using a variety of valid visual sources such as pictures, symbols, electronic media, print material, and artifacts.

15.B Create and interpret visuals, including pictures and maps.

Look at the pictures.
Tell about life in each place.

Teaching Note: Review what each photo shows. Encourage children to describe the shelter, the kinds of clothing people are wearing, and the kinds of food they are eating. Also discuss the activities and jobs pictured. After, encourage children to talk about what life is like in their community based on their geographic location.

Chapter 3

TEKS Practice

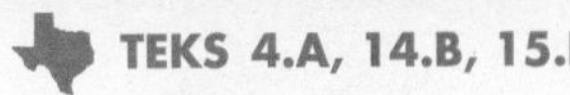

TEKS 4.A, 14.B, 15.B

1. Circle the correct word.

The playground is to the ________ of the school.

left right

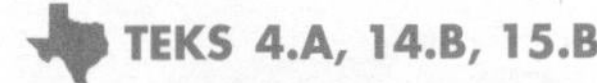

TEKS 4.A, 14.B, 15.B

2. Circle the correct word.

The lake is ________ the street.

over near far

TEKS 5.A, 14.B, 15.B

3. Write *L* on land.
Write *W* on water.

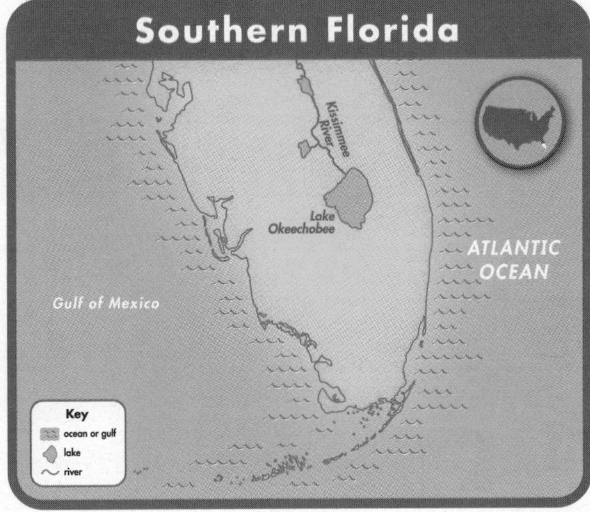

Chapter 3

TEKS Practice

TEKS 5.A, 14.B, 15.B

4. Match Draw a line from the word to a matching picture.

river

hill

mountain

ocean

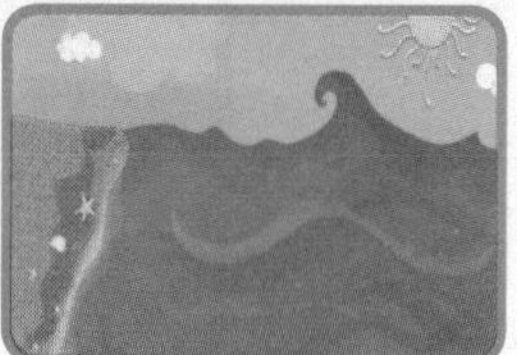

TEKS 5.A, 14.B, 15.B

5. Circle natural resources.

TEKS 5.A, 5.B, 14.B, 15.B

6. Classify and Categorize

Circle hot weather. **Circle** items you use in hot weather.

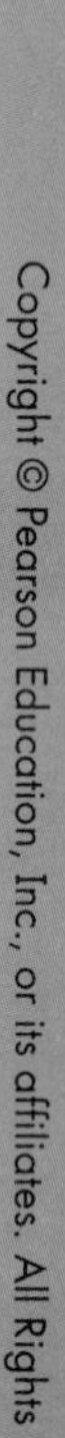

Chapter 3

TEKS Practice

 TEKS 5.A, 14.B, 15.B

7. Match Draw a line from the word to a matching picture.

rainy

hot

cold

TEKS 5.B, 14.B, 15.B

8. Circle an activity you can do in a hot place.

TEKS 5.B, 14.B, 15.B

9. Circle the names of foods you can eat in the place shown.

beans apples bananas
oranges corn potatoes

Texas Essential Knowledge and Skills

SS 15.B Create and interpret visuals, including pictures and maps.

ELA 13 Students use elements of the writing process (planning, drafting) to compose text.

my Story Book

Think of a place you would like to visit.
Draw a picture of what the place looks like.

Teaching Note: Read the prompt aloud. Brainstorm places and write them down. Then have children complete the activity. Encourage children to describe the completed drawing, and explain why they chose this place to picture.

Texas

Chapter 4

Our Traditions

THE BIG ? How is culture shared?

Teaching Note: Explain that *culture* means "how a group of people live." Add that culture includes kinds of food, music, art, language, clothing, shelter, and celebrations. Discuss the Chinese New Year parade in the photo, and point out that the people are carrying a model of a Chinese dragon.

PEARSON realize. Go online to access your interactive digital lesson.

Chapter 4

Our Traditions

Texas Essential Knowledge and Skills

15.B Create and interpret visuals, including pictures and maps.

my Story Spark

Think of your favorite food. **Draw** a picture of it.

Teaching Note: Read the prompt aloud. Brainstorm favorite foods with children. After their drawings are completed, talk about what children especially like about the favorite food they drew. Ask about any special times when this food is served, such as for a celebration.

Begin With a Song

Texas Essential Knowledge and Skills

1.B Identify customs associated with national patriotic holidays such as parades and fireworks on Independence Day.
14.A Obtain information about a topic using a variety of valid oral sources such as conversations, interviews, and music.
15.B Create and interpret visuals, including pictures and maps.

Holidays Are Special Days

Sing to the tune of "Yankee Doodle."

Holidays are special days
When families get together.
These are times we share good food
In any kind of weather!

There are times to have parades
Or have a celebration.
There are times to think about
Great people in our nation!

Teaching Note: Sing the song together as you point to the picture that goes with each part. Then talk about the Fourth of July celebration shown in the last picture. Explain that the figure is dressed as Uncle Sam, who is a symbol of our country. Ask children to describe other celebrations.

Chapter 4

Vocabulary Preview

Circle examples of these words in the picture.

family

custom

celebrate

holiday

tradition

culture

Teaching Note: Discuss the Fourth of July parade shown in the central picture. Ask children to identify Uncle Sam. Then point to and read aloud each word and discuss its meaning. Help children look for and circle an example of each word in the picture.

Texas

Lesson 1

How are people similar and different?

Texas Essential Knowledge and Skills

11.A Identify similarities and differences among people such as kinship, laws, and religion.

14.B Obtain information about a topic using a variety of valid visual sources such as pictures, symbols, electronic media, print material, and artifacts.

15.B Create and interpret visuals, including pictures and maps.

Sam and Lin are brother and sister.
Sam and Lin are similar, or like each other.
They are different, too.

Teaching Note: Read the text aloud. Discuss kinship, or how people are related. Point out that the children often look alike because they are brother and sister. Discuss other similarities, such as that both children are wearing glasses and holding balls. Then discuss differences, such as the color and sleeve length of the children's shirts.

Go online to access your interactive digital lesson.

Texas

Lesson 1

How are people similar and different?

Texas Essential Knowledge and Skills

11.A Identify similarities and differences among people such as kinship, laws, and religion.

14.B Obtain information about a topic using a variety of valid visual sources such as pictures, symbols, electronic media, print material, and artifacts.

15.B Create and interpret visuals, including pictures and maps.

Circle ways these sisters are like each other. **Draw** an X on ways they are different.

Teaching Note: Read the prompts aloud. First talk about how the two girls shown are similar because they are twin sisters. Then discuss how they are different. Point out that two items that are like each other, such as the shirts, can also be different, as in color. Then have children complete the activity.

Reading Skills: Compare and Contrast

TEKS

SS 11.A Identify similarities and differences among people such as kinship.

SS 15.B Interpret visuals, including pictures.

ELA 10.D Use illustrations to make predictions about text.

Some things are similar, or like each other.
Other things are different, or not like each other.

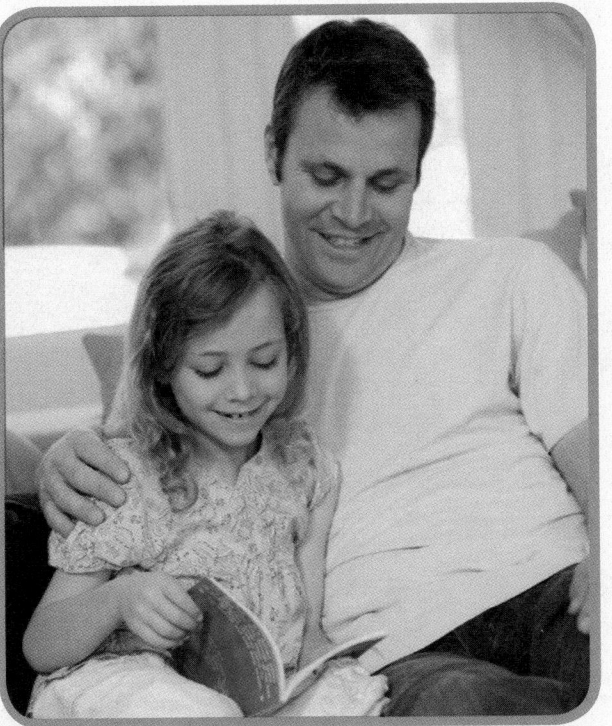

Teaching Note: Read the text aloud. Explain that when we compare, we see how things are similar. When we contrast, we see how things are different. Explain that the photos might show a mom and son and a dad and daughter. Then discuss how the relationships and activities are similar and different.

Reading Skills: Compare and Contrast

TEKS

SS 11.A Identify similarities and differences among people such as kinship.
SS 15.B Interpret visuals, including pictures.
ELA 10.D Use illustrations to make predictions about text.

Try it!

What do both pictures show?
Tell how they are similar and different.

Teaching Note: Read the prompts aloud. Have children tell you at least one example of a similarity and one example of a difference between the pictures. Then have children complete the activity. Discuss what children found when they are finished.

Texas

Lesson 2

How are families similar and different?

Texas Essential Knowledge and Skills

11.A Identify similarities and differences among people such as kinship, laws, and religion.

14.A Obtain information about a topic using a variety of valid oral sources such as conversations, interviews, and music.

14.B Obtain information about a topic using a variety of valid visual sources such as pictures, symbols, electronic media, print material, and artifacts.

15.B Create and interpret visuals, including pictures and maps.

There are different kinds of families. Families can be large or small, too.

Teaching Note: Point out that families can have one or more parents or children. Discuss kinship and how some families have grandparents, aunts, and uncles, and some families have children who are adopted. As children share information about their families, emphasize that each child is part of a family.

PEARSON realize. Go online to access your interactive digital lesson.

Texas

Lesson 2

How are families similar and different?

Texas Essential Knowledge and Skills

11.A Identify similarities and differences among people such as kinship, laws, and religion.

14.A Obtain information about a topic using a variety of valid oral sources such as conversations, interviews, and music.

14.B Obtain information about a topic using a variety of valid visual sources such as pictures, symbols, electronic media, print material, and artifacts.

15.B Create and interpret visuals, including pictures and maps.

Draw a picture of your family.
Talk about your family with a friend.

Teaching Note: Read the prompts aloud. Discuss children's relationships to family members, including siblings, parents, and grandparents. Then have them complete the activity. After, have children work in pairs to interview each other about similarities and differences between their families.

Texas

Lesson 3

What are our customs and traditions?

Families have different ways of doing things. We learn some of these ways from parents and grandparents.

Texas Essential Knowledge and Skills

11.B Identify similarities and differences among people such as music, clothing, and food.

12.A Describe and explain the importance of family customs and traditions.

12.B Compare family customs and traditions.

15.B Create and interpret visuals, including pictures and maps.

Teaching Note: Explain that people have special customs that are passed down over time and become traditions. Talk about the importance of family customs and traditions. Discuss similarities and differences in food, eating methods, and clothing in the pictures. Identify customs and traditions.

Go online to access your interactive digital lesson.

What are our customs and traditions?

Texas Essential Knowledge and Skills

11.B Identify similarities and differences among people such as music, clothing, and food.

12.A Describe and explain the importance of family customs and traditions.

12.B Compare family customs and traditions.

15.B Create and interpret visuals, including pictures and maps.

Draw a special day with your family. **Draw** the clothing that you wear and the food that you eat.

Teaching Note: Read the prompts aloud. Help children identify and explain the importance of the clothing and food customs and traditions their families share on special days. After children have finished their drawings, have them stand in a circle and tell how their family customs and traditions are similar and different.

Texas

Lesson 4

Who are American folk heroes?

Texas Essential Knowledge and Skills

14.B Obtain information about a topic using a variety of valid visual sources such as pictures, symbols, electronic media, print material, and artifacts.

15.A Express ideas orally based on knowledge and experiences.

15.B Create and interpret visuals, including pictures and maps.

We tell stories about our country and people in the past.

Betsy Ross

Johnny Appleseed

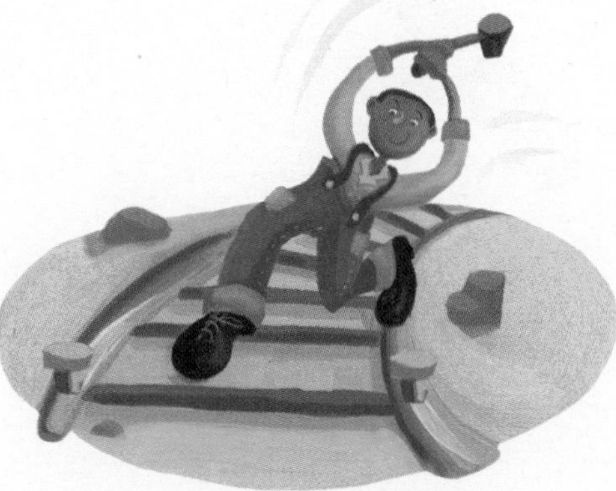

John Henry

Teaching Note: Read the text aloud. Explain that an American folk hero can be a real or make-believe person from the past. Discuss how telling stories about these people is a part of our cultural heritage, or way of life. Retell each story, and then have children talk about how each person is a good citizen.

Go online to access your interactive digital lesson.

Texas

Lesson 4

Who are American folk heroes?

Texas Essential Knowledge and Skills

14.B Obtain information about a topic using a variety of valid visual sources such as pictures, symbols, electronic media, print material, and artifacts.

15.A Express ideas orally based on knowledge and experiences.

15.B Create and interpret visuals, including pictures and maps.

Circle the picture that stands for your favorite folk hero. Then **retell** the story.

Teaching Note: Help children name each item pictured and associate it with one of the folk heroes from the previous page. Then ask them to pick an item that belongs to their favorite folk hero and retell the story heard from the first page. Ask why this folk hero is their favorite.

21C

Critical Thinking: Distinguish Fact From Fiction

TEKS

SS 15.B Interpret visuals, including pictures.
ELA 6.A Identify elements of a story.
ELA 10.D Use illustrations to make predictions about text.

A fact is true. Fiction is made up.

Abraham Lincoln was a United States president.

fact

Jack climbed a giant beanstalk.

fiction

Teaching Note: Read aloud the text and examples of fact and fiction. Discuss the pictures as you encourage children to look for factual and fictional details. Explain that Abraham Lincoln was a real person and a United States president. Point out that beanstalks are real, but stalks as big as the one shown are make-believe.

PEARSON realize. Go online to access your interactive digital lesson.

21C

Critical Thinking: Distinguish Fact From Fiction

TEKS

SS 15.B Interpret visuals, including pictures.
ELA 6.A Identify elements of a story.
ELA 10.D Use illustrations to make predictions about text.

Try it!

Circle the picture that shows a fact.

Paul Bunyan was as tall as a tree.

George Washington was our first president.

Teaching Note: Remind children of the meaning of *fact* and *fiction*. Discuss what the pictures show and then read each sentence aloud. Have them complete the activity and explain their picture choice.

Texas

Lesson 5

What are different religions?

> **Texas Essential Knowledge and Skills**
>
> **11.A** Identify similarities and differences among people such as kinship, laws, and religion.
>
> **14.B** Obtain information about a topic using a variety of valid visual sources such as pictures, symbols, electronic media, print material, and artifacts.
>
> **15.B** Create and interpret visuals, including pictures and maps.

There are many different religions.
They have their own customs and traditions.
Some have special celebrations and holidays.

Teaching Note: Be sensitive to children's beliefs as you discuss religion. Explain that most religions include ideas about God. They have rules, responsibilities, and places where people meet to express their beliefs. The photos show a Christian church, a Buddhist temple, a Muslim mosque, and a Jewish synagogue.

Go online to access your interactive digital lesson.

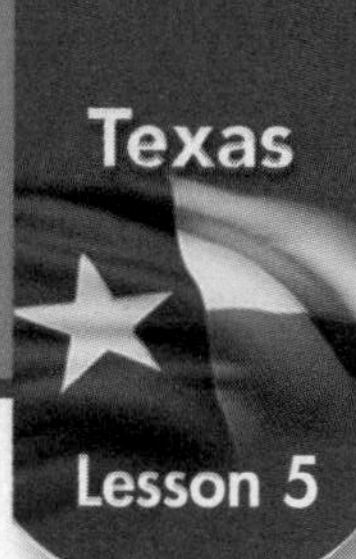

Texas

Lesson 5

What are different religions?

Texas Essential Knowledge and Skills

11.A Identify similarities and differences among people such as kinship, laws, and religion.

14.B Obtain information about a topic using a variety of valid visual sources such as pictures, symbols, electronic media, print material, and artifacts.

15.B Create and interpret visuals, including pictures and maps.

Draw a place in your community.
Show where people meet to practice religion.

Teaching Note: Read the prompts aloud. Brainstorm ideas about places of worship in the community. Encourage children to say what they know about each one and to describe what the buildings look like. Then have children complete the activity.

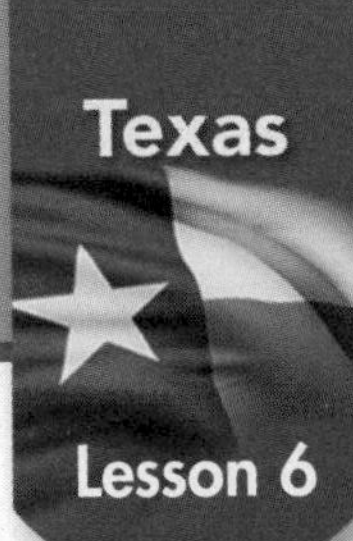

How do families celebrate?

Texas Essential Knowledge and Skills

12.A Describe and explain the importance of family customs and traditions.
12.B Compare family customs and traditions.
15.B Create and interpret visuals, including pictures and maps.

Families celebrate special days.
Families celebrate in many ways.

Teaching Note: Talk about the kinds of celebrations shown in the photos (quinceañera, graduation, wedding). Ask children to describe celebrations or special days they have been a part of. Discuss the importance of these customs and traditions and the different ways people celebrate them.

Go online to access your interactive digital lesson.

How do families celebrate?

Texas Essential Knowledge and Skills

12.A Describe and explain the importance of family customs and traditions.

12.B Compare family customs and traditions.

15.B Create and interpret visuals, including pictures and maps.

Color what you use to celebrate.

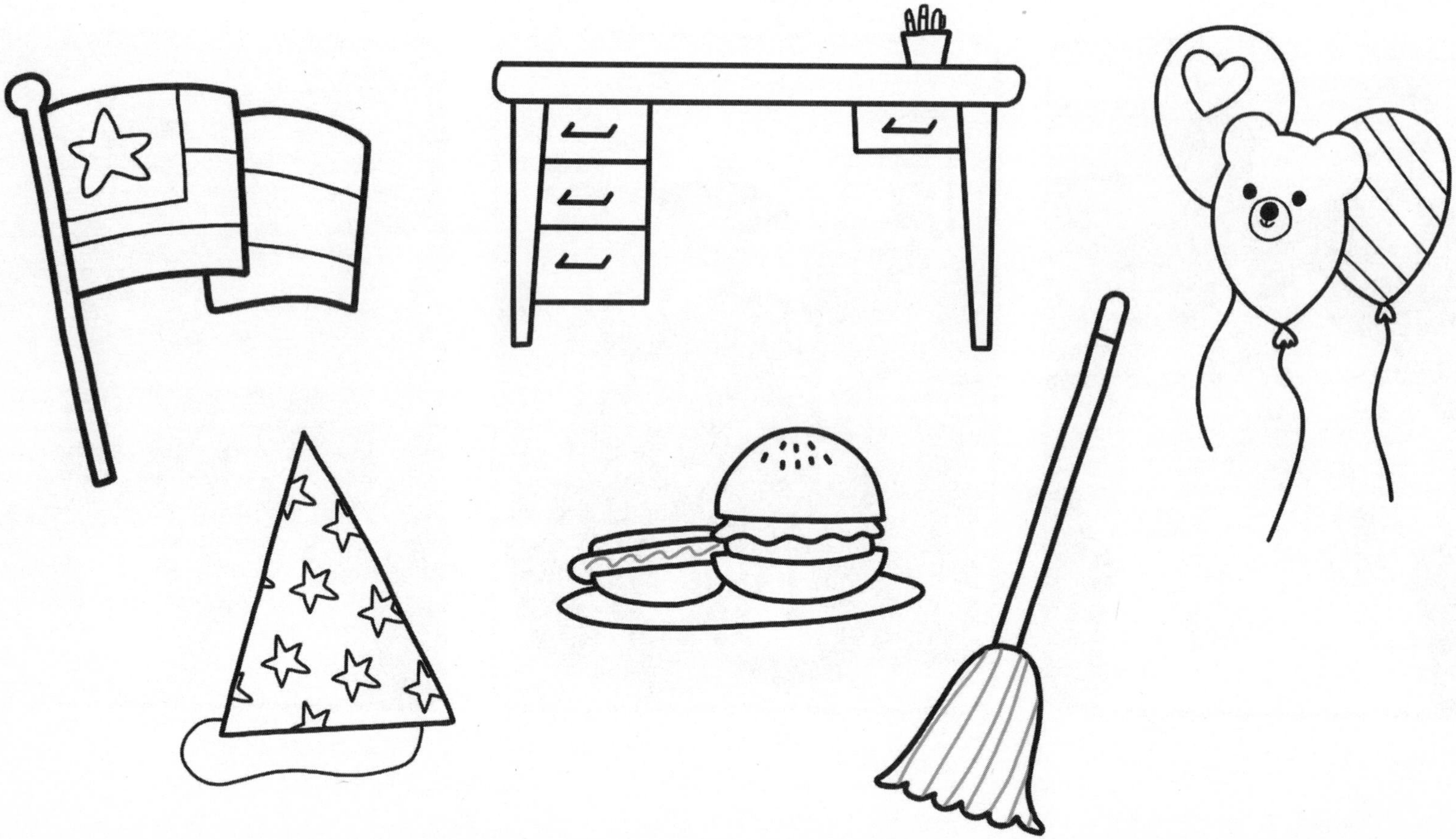

Teaching Note: Read the prompt aloud. Discuss the different items people use in celebrations. Then have children complete the activity. Ask them to describe and explain the importance of family customs and traditions.

What are national holidays?

We remember people and events when we celebrate holidays.

Texas Essential Knowledge and Skills

1.A Explain the reasons for national patriotic holidays such as Presidents' Day, Veterans Day, and Independence Day.

1.B Identify customs associated with national patriotic holidays such as parades and fireworks on Independence Day.

14.B Obtain information about a topic using a variety of valid visual sources such as pictures, symbols, electronic media, print material, and artifacts.

15.B Create and interpret visuals, including pictures and maps.

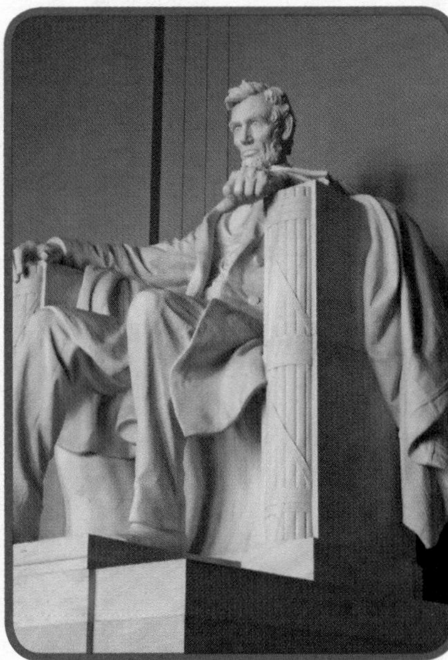

Teaching Note: Name different U.S. national holidays, such as Presidents' Day, Veterans Day, and Independence Day. Talk about the events and people that are remembered on each day. Point out special customs and traditions that are part of holiday celebrations, such as parades and fireworks.

PEARSON realize™ Go online to access your interactive digital lesson.

Texas

Lesson 7

What are national holidays?

Texas Essential Knowledge and Skills

1.A Explain the reasons for national patriotic holidays such as Presidents' Day, Veterans Day, and Independence Day.

1.B Identify customs associated with national patriotic holidays such as parades and fireworks on Independence Day.

14.B Obtain information about a topic using a variety of valid visual sources such as pictures, symbols, electronic media, print material, and artifacts.

15.B Create and interpret visuals, including pictures and maps.

Draw a line to match each picture to a sentence.

We celebrate our country.

We remember our brave leaders.

We show respect for our soldiers.

Teaching Note: Talk about what children see in each picture and what holiday is represented. Have children say why we celebrate each one. Then read each sentence aloud, and have children draw a line to match the sentence to a picture. Discuss the customs and traditions that are associated with each holiday.

What is culture?

Texas Essential Knowledge and Skills

11.B Identify similarities and differences among people such as music, clothing, and food.

14.B Obtain information about a topic using a variety of valid visual sources such as pictures, symbols, electronic media, print material, and artifacts.

15.A Express ideas orally based on knowledge and experiences.

15.B Create and interpret visuals, including pictures and maps.

Culture is the way a group of people live. There are many cultures around the world.

Teaching Note: Discuss similarities and differences in the clothing, instruments, and activities pictured. Talk about the ways people express themselves through music, dancing, and telling stories. Discuss the different kinds of musical instruments people play, and the clothing people wear. Have children tell about their culture.

Go online to access your interactive digital lesson.

Texas

Lesson 8

What is culture?

Texas Essential Knowledge and Skills

11.B Identify similarities and differences among people such as music, clothing, and food.

14.B Obtain information about a topic using a variety of valid visual sources such as pictures, symbols, electronic media, print material, and artifacts.

15.B Create and interpret visuals, including pictures and maps.

Color the things that you know.

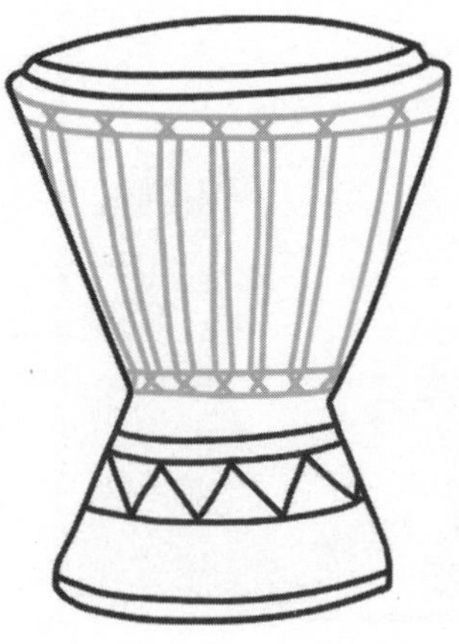

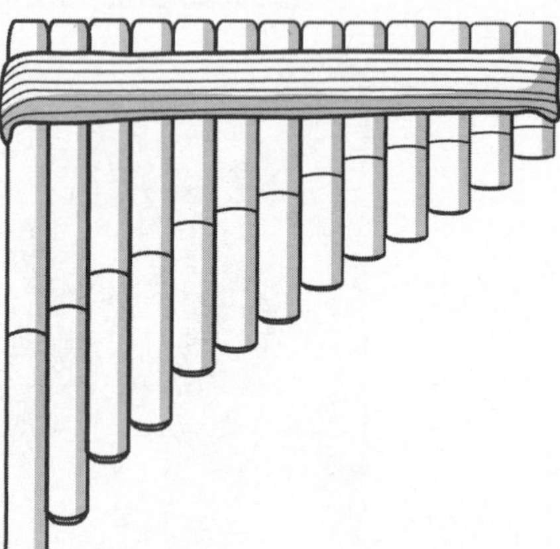

Teaching Note: Read the prompt aloud. Talk about the pictures, and have children identify the items as clothing and musical instruments from different cultures. Then have them complete the activity. Ask what children know about the pictures they colored.

Chapter 4

TEKS Practice

TEKS 1.A

1. **Circle** What holiday celebrates United States soldiers?

Independence Day

Veterans Day

Presidents' Day

TEKS 1.A, 15.B

2. **Match** Draw a line from the words to a matching picture.

Independence Day

Presidents' Day

TEKS 1.B, 15.B

3. **Circle** What holiday custom does the picture show?

fireworks on Independence Day

parade on Veterans Day

dinner on Thanksgiving Day

Chapter 4

TEKS Practice

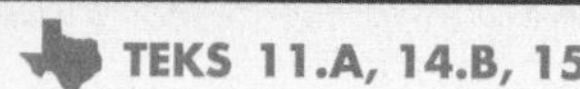

TEKS 11.A, 14.B, 15.B

4. **Compare and Contrast**

Circle What is one way these families are similar, or like each other?

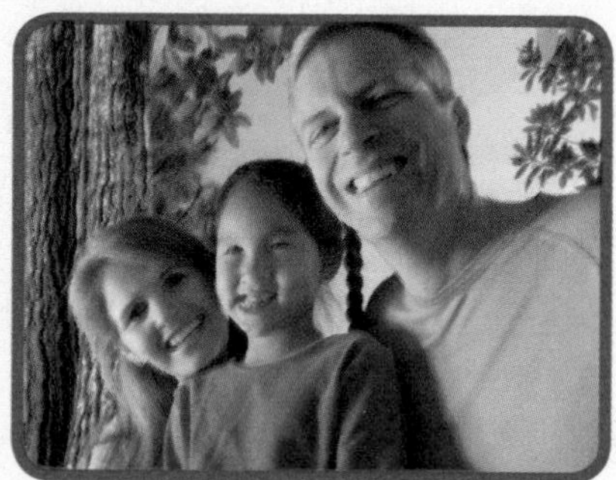

They have one child.

They have one parent.

They live in one house.

TEKS 11.B, 14.B, 15.B

5. **Circle** What is one way these children are different, or not like each other?

the clothes they are wearing

the color of their hair

what they are doing

Chapter 4

TEKS Practice

TEKS 11.B, 15.B

6. **Circle** What is one way these items are similar, or like each other?

You can eat them.

You can wear them.

You can listen to them.

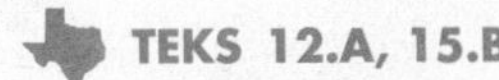

TEKS 12.A, 15.B

7. **Circle** What picture shows a family custom or tradition?

TEKS 14.B, 15.B

8. **Match** Draw a line from each family custom or tradition to a matching picture.

special event

eating together

shared activity

helping each other

my Story Book

Texas Essential Knowledge and Skills

SS 15.B Create visuals, including pictures.

ELA 13 Students use elements of the writing process (planning, drafting) to compose text.

Think of something you celebrate.
Draw a picture of what you do.

Teaching Note: Read the prompt aloud. Talk about the different celebrations shown in the lessons and other celebrations children are familiar with. Ask them to think of a celebration they take part in and draw what happens at that event. Ask children to describe their final pictures.

Go online to access your interactive digital lesson.

Texas

Chapter

5

Life Then and Now

THE BIG ? How does life change throughout history?

Teaching Note: Read the chapter title and the Big Question. Talk about the meaning of *history* as "events that happen over time." Use the photos as examples of how children's dress and hairstyles have changed over time. Explain that every person has his or her own history.

PEARSON realize. Go online to access your interactive digital lesson.

Chapter 5

Life Then and Now

Texas Essential Knowledge and Skills

15.B Create and interpret visuals, including pictures and maps.

my Story Spark

Draw a picture of yourself when you were little.
Then **draw** a picture of yourself now.

Teaching Note: Read the prompts aloud. Ask children to think about what they looked like as babies and as toddlers. Discuss what has changed, such as height and type of clothes, and what has stayed the same, such as color of hair and eyes.

Begin With a Song

Texas Essential Knowledge and Skills

14.A Obtain information about a topic using a variety of valid oral sources such as conversations, interviews, and music.

15.B Create and interpret visuals, including pictures and maps.

We Share History

Sing to the tune of "Twinkle, Twinkle, Little Star."

Study all your history.
Learn about the past with me.
Study customs of each kind.
Study artifacts you find.
Study landmarks everywhere.
History is what we share!

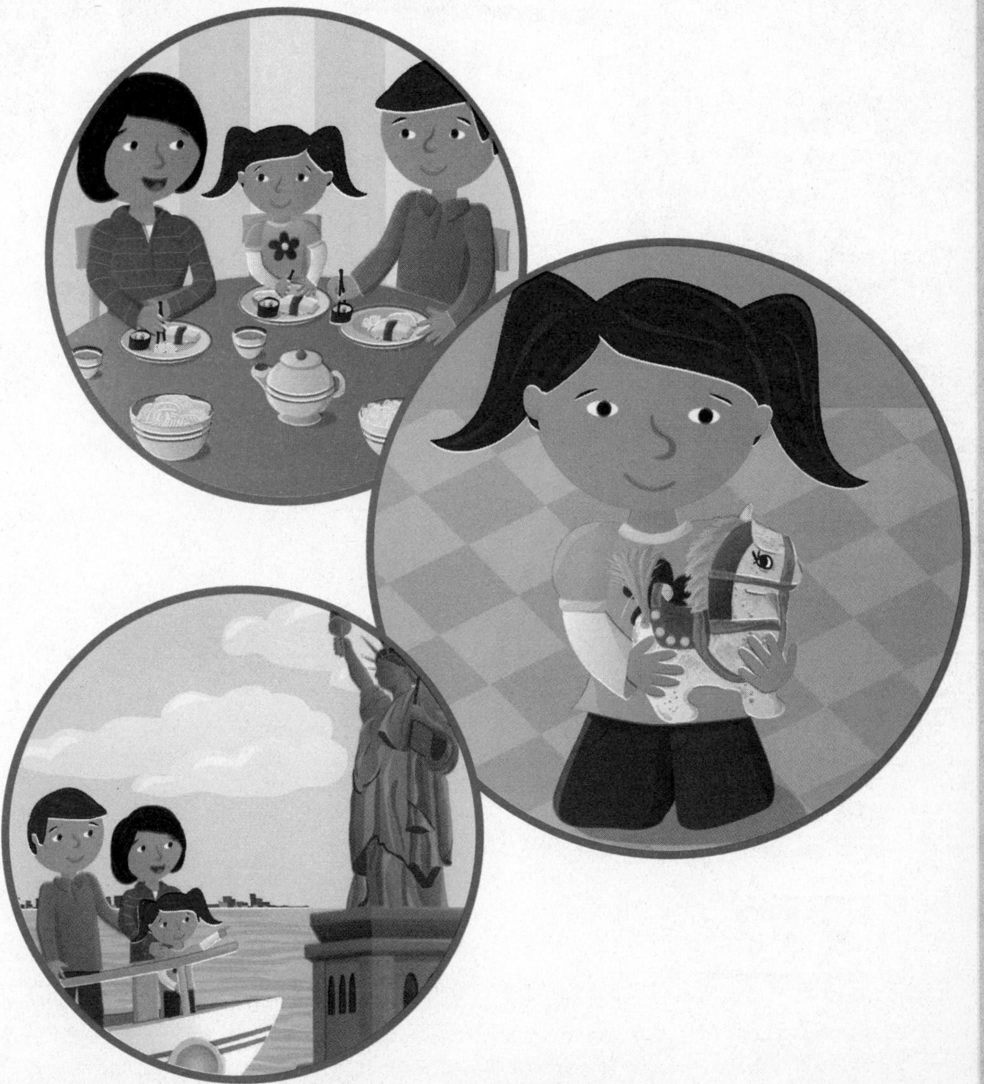

Teaching Note: Sing the song, and point to the pictures. Review the meanings of *history* and *customs*. Explain that *artifacts* are things, such as tools and toys, that people make. Point out that artifacts can be used to learn about history. Then point to the Statue of Liberty. Explain that this landmark is part of our country's history.

Chapter 5

Vocabulary Preview

Circle examples of these words in the picture.

picture

calendar

timeline

past

hero

community

Teaching Note: Discuss the classroom scene shown in the central picture. Ask children to point out and name objects. Then read each word aloud, and talk about the photo. Help children find and circle an example of each word in the picture.

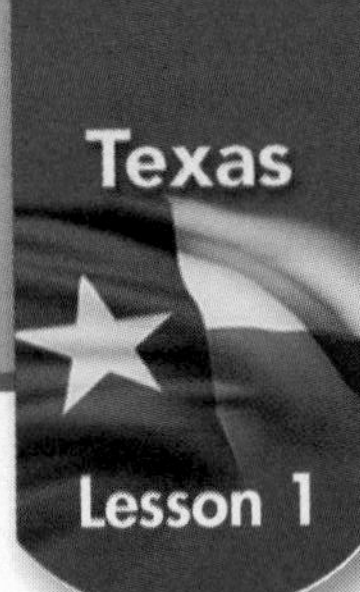

What is my personal history?

Texas Essential Knowledge and Skills

14.B Obtain information about a topic using a variety of valid visual sources such as pictures, symbols, electronic media, print material, and artifacts.

15.B Create and interpret visuals, including pictures and maps.

History is the story of the past.
We all have a history.

Teaching Note: Read the lesson title and the text. Explain that *personal* means "something that relates to a person." Discuss the kinds of chronological events that are a part of everyone's personal history, such as the first day of school. Point to the pictures. Ask children to tell what they learned to do at each stage of life.

PEARSON realize **Go online to access your interactive digital lesson.**

What is my personal history?

Texas Essential Knowledge and Skills

14.B Obtain information about a topic using a variety of valid visual sources such as pictures, symbols, electronic media, print material, and artifacts.

15.B Create and interpret visuals, including pictures and maps.

Circle in blue things you may have used as a baby.
Circle in red things you may use today.

Teaching Note: Read the prompts aloud. Help children identify the objects shown on the page. Discuss which things would be used by a baby and which by an older child. Then provide blue and red crayons, and have children complete the activity. Discuss their choices.

Reading Skills: Sequence

TEKS

SS 3.A Place events in chronological order.

SS 3.B Use vocabulary related to chronology, including next, first, and last.

SS 14.C Sequence and categorize information.

ELA 10.C Discuss the ways authors group information in text.

You can use **first, next,** and **last** to show the order of when things happen.

first

next

last

Teaching Note: Read the text aloud. Then talk about the pictures. Ask: *What does the girl do first to get ready for school? What does she do next? What does she do last?* Help children use *first, next,* and *last* to talk about the order of events in a school activity.

PEARSON realize. Go online to access your interactive digital lesson.

Reading Skills: Sequence

TEKS

SS 3.A Place events in chronological order.
SS 3.B Use vocabulary related to chronology, including next, first, and last.
SS 14.C Sequence and categorize information.
ELA 10.C Discuss the ways authors group information in text.

Look at the pictures.
Write first, next, or **last** under each picture to show the order.

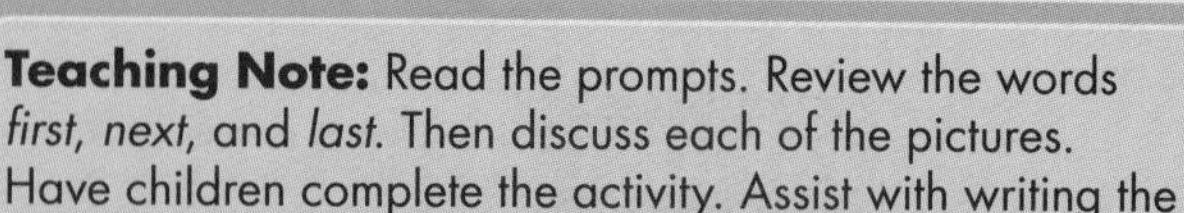

Teaching Note: Read the prompts. Review the words *first, next,* and *last.* Then discuss each of the pictures. Have children complete the activity. Assist with writing the words as necessary. Ask them to share how they ordered the pictures.

Texas

Lesson 2

How do we talk about time?

Texas Essential Knowledge and Skills

3.B Use vocabulary related to time and chronology, including before, after, next, first, last, yesterday, today, and tomorrow.

14.B Obtain information about a topic using a variety of valid visual sources such as pictures, symbols, electronic media, print material, and artifacts.

15.B Create and interpret visuals, including pictures and maps.

We can use **before, now,** and **after** to tell about time.

before

now

after

Teaching Note: Use the word *before, now,* or *after* to talk about each photo. Ask: *What happens before the children play music? What are the children doing now? What happens after the children play music?* Discuss the order of another classroom activity using *before, now,* and *after.*

PEARSON realize — Go online to access your interactive digital lesson.

How do we talk about time?

Texas Essential Knowledge and Skills

3.B Use vocabulary related to time and chronology, including before, after, next, first, last, yesterday, today, and tomorrow.
14.B Obtain information about a topic using a variety of valid visual sources such as pictures, symbols, electronic media, print material, and artifacts.
15.B Create and interpret visuals, including pictures and maps.

Look at each picture.
Draw a picture to show what the girl would do after she paints.
Tell about your picture.

before

now

after

Teaching Note: Read the prompts, and discuss what the girl is doing in the two pictures. Point to the words beneath the pictures, and say each one. Explain that these are just some of the words that we use to talk about time. Have children complete the activity and then describe what they drew.

Texas

Lesson 3

How do we measure time?

Texas Essential Knowledge and Skills

3.B Use vocabulary related to time and chronology, including before, after, next, first, last, yesterday, today, and tomorrow.

14.B Obtain information about a topic using a variety of valid visual sources such as pictures, symbols, electronic media, print material, and artifacts.

15.B Create and interpret visuals, including pictures and maps.

A calendar shows days of the week and months of the year. We can use **yesterday, today,** and **tomorrow** to tell about time.

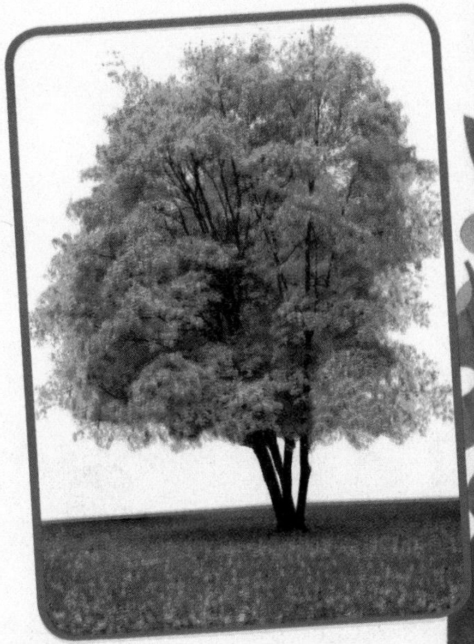

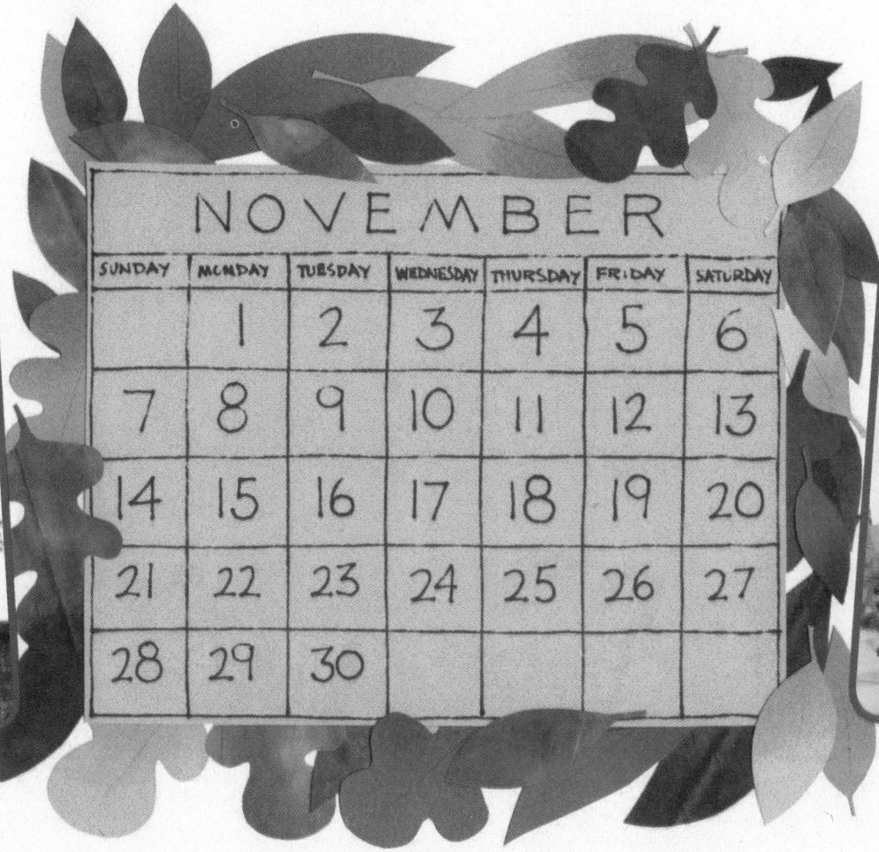

NOVEMBER

SUNDAY	MONDAY	TUESDAY	WEDNESDAY	THURSDAY	FRIDAY	SATURDAY
	1	2	3	4	5	6
7	8	9	10	11	12	13
14	15	16	17	18	19	20
21	22	23	24	25	26	27
28	29	30				

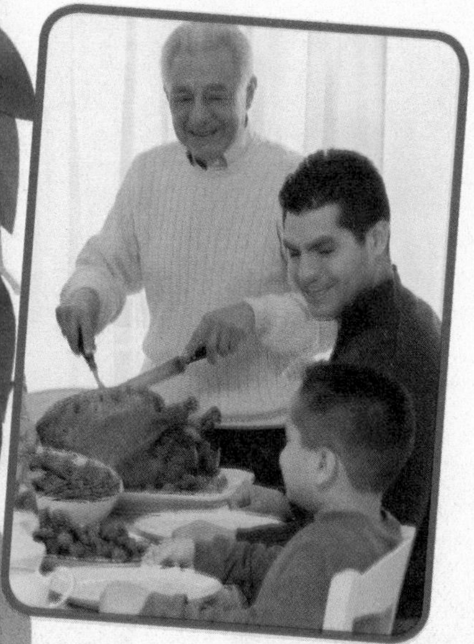

Teaching Note: Explain that the central picture is a calendar page for November. Read the names of the days, and explain that there are 30 days in this month. Then point to November 3. Say: *If today is Wednesday, November 3, what will tomorrow be?* Explain that a calendar is a good source for obtaining information.

Go online to access your interactive digital lesson.

How do we measure time?

Texas Essential Knowledge and Skills

3.B Use vocabulary related to time and chronology, including before, after, next, first, last, yesterday, today, and tomorrow.

14.B Obtain information about a topic using a variety of valid visual sources such as pictures, symbols, electronic media, print material, and artifacts.

15.B Create and interpret visuals, including pictures and maps.

Draw something you will do this month.
Tell about your picture.

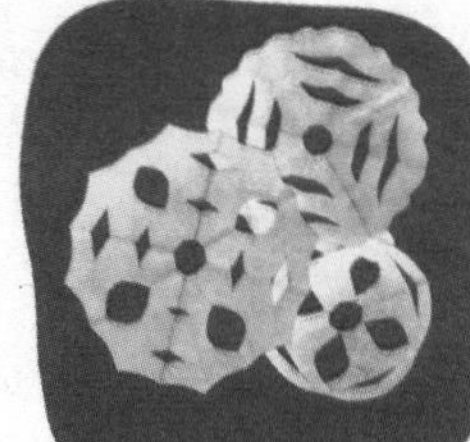

Teaching Note: Read the prompt aloud. Help children associate a month with each of the pictures on the page. Talk about the current month and what activities they like to do. When drawings are finished, ask children to tell about the activity using a time word such as *yesterday, today,* or *tomorrow.*

What is a timeline?

Texas Essential Knowledge and Skills

3.A Place events in chronological order.
14.B Obtain information about a topic using a variety of valid visual sources such as pictures, symbols, electronic media, print material, and artifacts.
14.C Sequence and categorize information.
15.B Create and interpret visuals, including pictures and maps.

A timeline shows the order in which things happen.

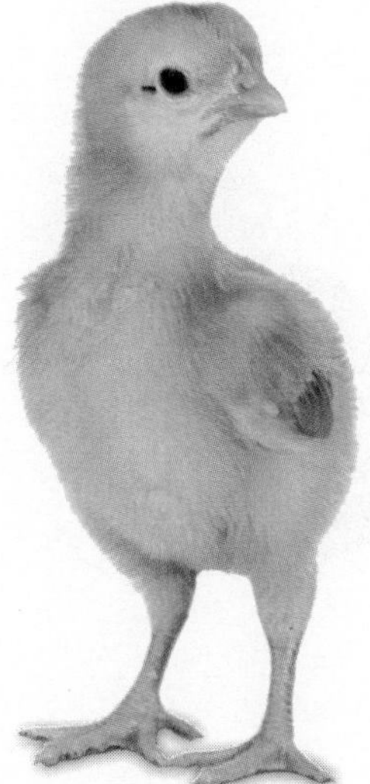

1 2 3

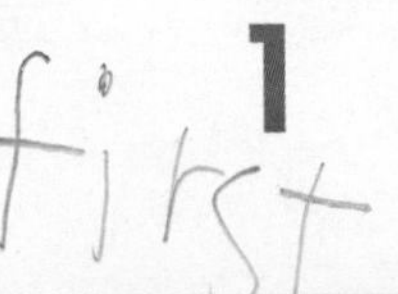

last

Teaching Note: Trace the line from left to right with your finger. Explain that a timeline shows changes over time starting with the earliest picture on the left. Talk about chronology and how the chick grows and changes from hatching at number 1 to a young chick at number 2 to a full-grown chicken at number 3.

Go online to access your interactive digital lesson.

What is a timeline?

Texas Essential Knowledge and Skills

3.A Place events in chronological order.
14.B Obtain information about a topic using a variety of valid visual sources such as pictures, symbols, electronic media, print material, and artifacts.
14.C Sequence and categorize information.
15.B Create and interpret visuals, including pictures and maps.

Show where the pictures go on the timeline.
Draw a line from each picture to a number.

1　　2　　3

Teaching Note: Read the prompts aloud, and discuss the photos. Explain that two of the photos are out of order on the timeline. Have children complete the activity by putting the pictures in chronological order. Then talk about what children marked on the timeline for numbers 1, 2, and 3.

How can we learn about history?

Texas Essential Knowledge and Skills

14.A Obtain information about a topic using a variety of valid oral sources such as conversations, interviews, and music.

14.B Obtain information about a topic using a variety of valid visual sources such as pictures, symbols, electronic media, print material, and artifacts.

15.B Create and interpret visuals, including pictures and maps.

We can listen to stories about the past.
We can look at pictures and things from the past.

Teaching Note: Review the meaning of *history*. Use the photos to talk about ways we learn about the past, such as conversations or interviews with family members, photos, and artifacts. Bring in artifacts such as old toys for children to study. Ask children to tell about how they have learned about their history.

Go online to access your interactive digital lesson.

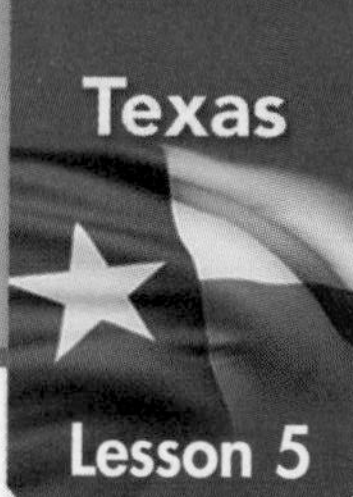

How can we learn about history?

Texas Essential Knowledge and Skills

14.A Obtain information about a topic using a variety of valid oral sources such as conversations, interviews, and music.

14.B Obtain information about a topic using a variety of valid visual sources such as pictures, symbols, electronic media, print material, and artifacts.

15.B Create and interpret visuals, including pictures and maps.

Circle ways we can learn about history.

Teaching Note: Read the prompt, and review the different ways to learn about history shown on the first page of the lesson, such as having a conversation with someone or looking at artifacts. Then have children complete the activity. After, have children tell ways they have learned about their family history.

21C

Critical Thinking: Use Illustrations

TEKS

SS 14.B Obtain information about a topic using visual sources such as pictures.

SS 15.B Interpret visuals, including pictures.

ELA 10.A Identify the topic and details in expository text, referring to the words and illustrations.

ELA 10.D Use illustrations to make predictions about text.

Pictures can show what a sentence tells.

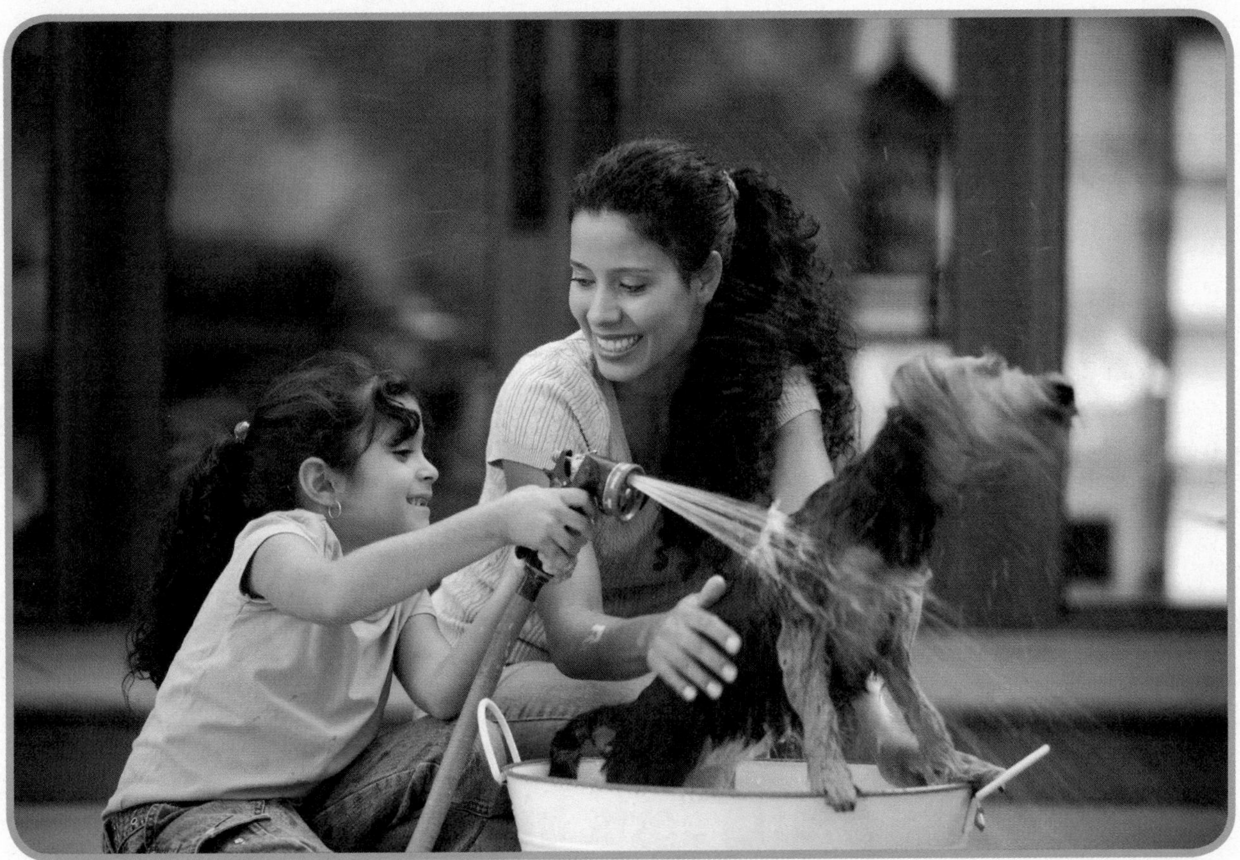

Jen washes her dog.

Teaching Note: Read the instructional text aloud. Then discuss what is shown in the picture. Read aloud the sentence, and ask children if it tells about the picture. Talk about how a picture can illustrate text and text can tell more about a picture.

Critical Thinking: Use Illustrations

TEKS

SS 14.B Obtain information about a topic using visual sources such as pictures.

SS 15.B Interpret visuals, including pictures.

ELA 10.A Identify the topic and details in expository text, referring to the words and illustrations.

ELA 10.D Use illustrations to make predictions about text.

Circle the picture that shows what the sentence says.

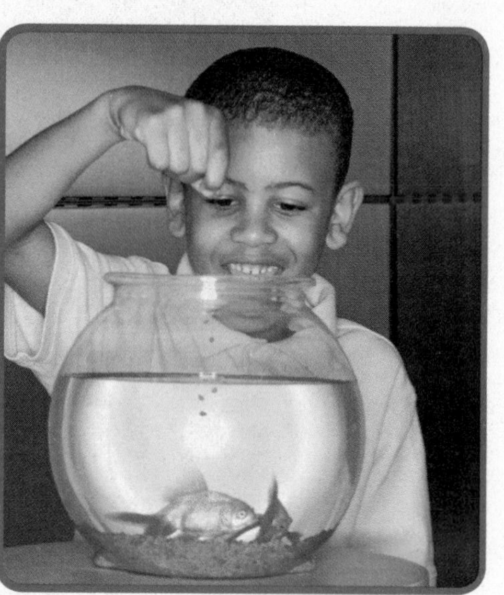

Matt feeds his fish.

Teaching Note: Read the prompt and the sentence below the pictures. Make sure children understand that they are to circle the picture that illustrates what the sentence says. Discuss why the other two pictures do not illustrate the sentence.

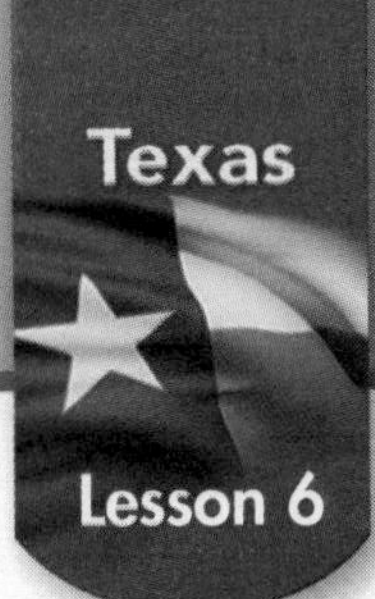

Who are explorers from the past?

Texas Essential Knowledge and Skills

2.A Identify contributions of historical figures, including Stephen F. Austin, George Washington, Christopher Columbus, and José Antonio Navarro, who helped to shape the state and nation.

14.B Obtain information about a topic using a variety of valid visual sources such as pictures, symbols, electronic media, print material, and artifacts.

An explorer travels.
An explorer looks for new places.

Teaching Note: Read the text aloud. Help children identify Sacagawea and Christopher Columbus. Tell about each explorer's life. Then relate how each person was an explorer looking for new places. Discuss other explorers from the past that children have heard about.

Go online to access your interactive digital lesson.

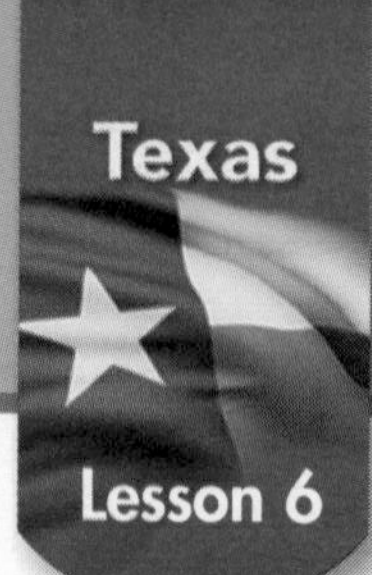

Who are explorers from the past?

Texas Essential Knowledge and Skills

2.A Identify contributions of historical figures, including Stephen F. Austin, George Washington, Christopher Columbus, and José Antonio Navarro, who helped to shape the state and nation.

14.B Obtain information about a topic using a variety of valid visual sources such as pictures, symbols, electronic media, print material, and artifacts.

Circle a picture. **Tell** the explorer's story.

Teaching Note: Point out to children that the pictures on the page are the same people that were shown on the first page of the lesson. Have children circle one picture and then take turns retelling that person's story and telling how he or she was an explorer. Encourage children to tell about a contribution he or she made.

Texas
Lesson 7

Who are American heroes from the past?

A hero works to help others.

Texas Essential Knowledge and Skills

2.A Identify contributions of historical figures, including Stephen F. Austin, George Washington, Christopher Columbus, and José Antonio Navarro, who helped to shape the state and nation.

14.B Obtain information about a topic using a variety of valid visual sources such as pictures, symbols, electronic media, print material, and artifacts.

15.B Create and interpret visuals, including pictures and maps.

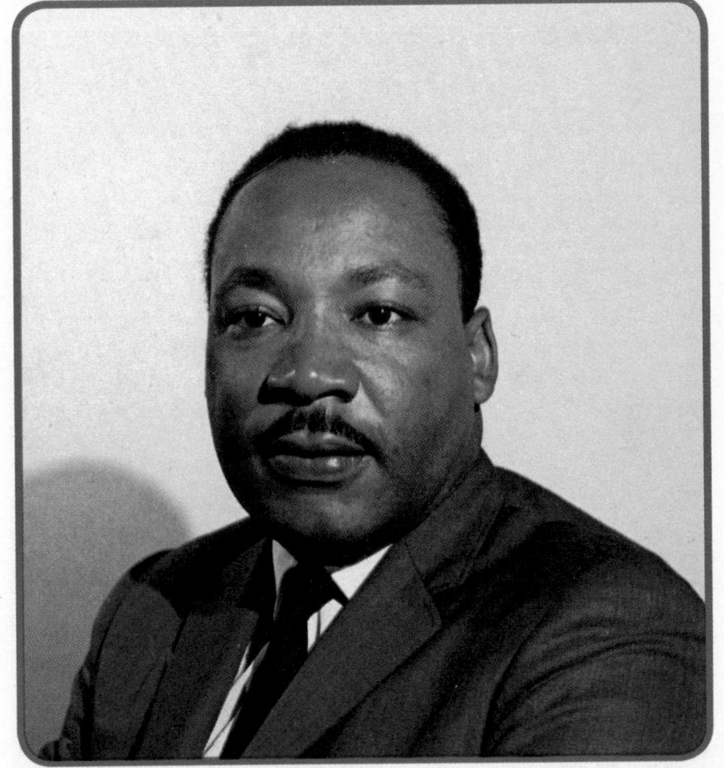

Teaching Note: Help children identify the person in each picture. Then relate why each person is considered a hero. Explain that Washington was a patriot who fought for his country, and King was a patriot who fought for people's rights. Discuss how each hero contributed to our nation and helped to shape it.

PEARSON realize Go online to access your interactive digital lesson.

Texas Lesson 7

Who are American heroes from the past?

Texas Essential Knowledge and Skills

2.A Identify contributions of historical figures, including Stephen F. Austin, George Washington, Christopher Columbus, and José Antonio Navarro, who helped to shape the state and nation.

14.B Obtain information about a topic using a variety of valid visual sources such as pictures, symbols, electronic media, print material, and artifacts.

15.B Create and interpret visuals, including pictures and maps.

Circle a picture of an American hero from the past.
Tell the hero's story.

Teaching Note: Point out to children that the pictures on the page are the same people that were shown on the first page of the lesson. Have children circle one picture. Then help them retell that person's story including how he was a hero and a patriot who contributed to our nation and helped to shape it.

Texas

Lesson 8

How has school changed?

Texas Essential Knowledge and Skills

13.A Identify examples of technology used in the home and school.

15.B Create and interpret visuals, including pictures and maps.

Some things about school change. Some things stay the same. Children now sit in groups to read. They still put up a hand to speak.

then

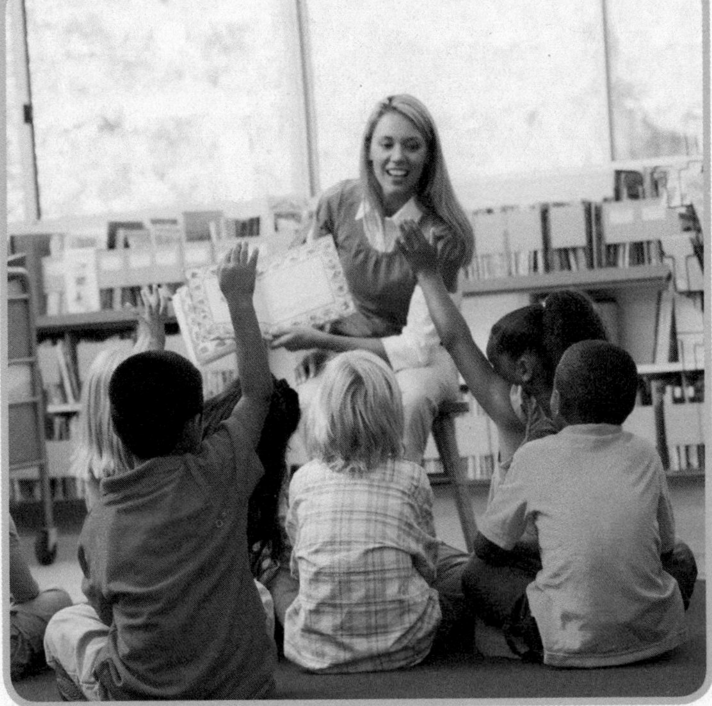

now

Teaching Note: Talk about ways school has changed and stayed the same from the past to now. Use the photos and the words *then* and *now* to illustrate ideas. Discuss examples of technology that children use in the classroom today and what children used long ago when these things did not exist.

How has school changed?

Texas Essential Knowledge and Skills

13.A Identify examples of technology used in the home and school.

15.B Create and interpret visuals, including pictures and maps.

Circle things that were used in schools long ago.

Teaching Note: Read the prompt aloud. Help children describe each picture and complete the activity. Ask them to explain their choices for things used long ago in schools. Talk about what it might have been like to write on a slate with chalk instead of using electronic media, such as a computer.

Texas

Lesson 9

How has the world changed?

Texas Essential Knowledge and Skills

14.B Obtain information about a topic using a variety of valid visual sources such as pictures, symbols, electronic media, print material, and artifacts.

15.B Create and interpret visuals, including pictures and maps.

Some things about communities change.
Some things stay the same.
There are new buildings. Today, people use cars.

then

now

Teaching Note: Review the meaning of *community*. Then read the text aloud, and discuss how communities can change and stay the same. Have children compare the community in the "then" and "now" pictures and point out similarities and differences, including technology that people did not have in the past, such as cars.

PEARSON realize. Go online to access your interactive digital lesson.

Texas
Lesson 9

How has the world changed?

Texas Essential Knowledge and Skills

14.B Obtain information about a topic using a variety of valid visual sources such as pictures, symbols, electronic media, print material, and artifacts.

15.B Create and interpret visuals, including pictures and maps.

Look at the pictures of the same place then and now.
Circle what is different in the picture that shows now.

then

now

Teaching Note: Read the prompt. Then have children compare the two community pictures and circle the differences in the "now" picture. After children have finished, discuss their choices. Compare the pictures, and point out any additional differences, including technological advances, such as the cell phone.

Texas

Lesson 10

How has technology changed?

Texas Essential Knowledge and Skills

13.A Identify examples of technology used in the home and school.

13.C Describe how his or her life might be different without modern technology.

14.B Obtain information about a topic using a variety of valid visual sources such as pictures, symbols, electronic media, print material, and artifacts.

15.A Express ideas orally based on knowledge and experiences.

The tools and machines we use have changed from the past.

then

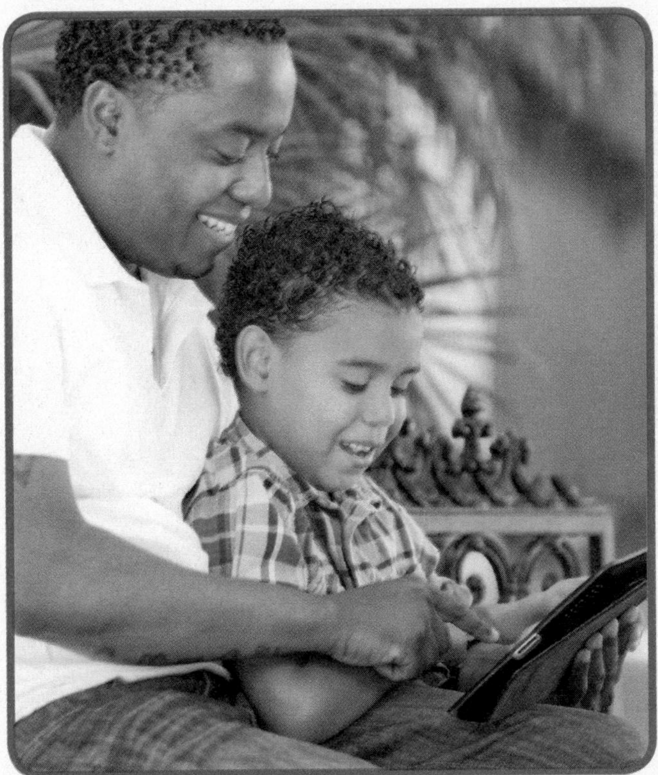

now

Teaching Note: Define *technology* as the tools and machines, such as computers, that people use for work and play. Read the text aloud, and discuss the photos. Talk about electronic media in the home, and how we can obtain information when we use it. Discuss how life would be different without it.

PEARSON realize | Go online to access your interactive digital lesson.

Texas

Lesson 10

How has technology changed?

Texas Essential Knowledge and Skills

13.A Identify examples of technology used in the home and school.

13.C Describe how his or her life might be different without modern technology.

14.B Obtain information about a topic using a variety of valid visual sources such as pictures, symbols, electronic media, print material, and artifacts.

15.A Express ideas orally based on knowledge and experiences.

Circle a tool or machine.
Tell what life would be like without it.

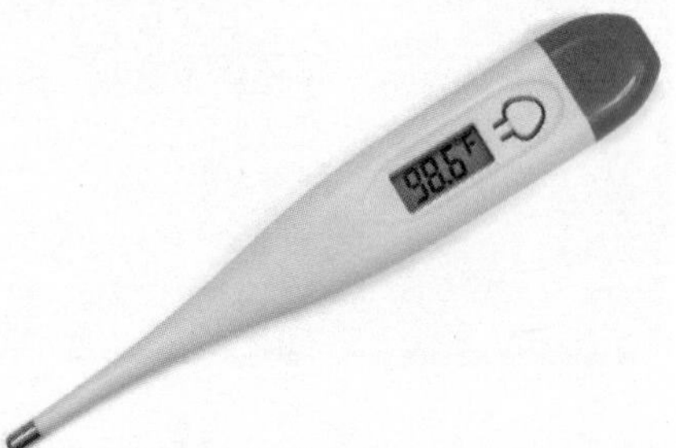

Teaching Note: Read the prompts. Discuss the pictures, and make sure that children recognize each kind of technology and how it meets our needs and wants. Have children complete the activity and then tell how their lives would be different without this tool or machine.

Chapter 5

TEKS Practice

TEKS 3.B, 14.C

1. Write B for **before. Write A** for **after.**

TEKS 3.B, 14.C

2. Sequence **Write F** for **first. Write N** for **next. Write L** for **last.**

TEKS 3.B

3. Circle words that tell about time.

school	yesterday	before
today	home	friends
after	flag	tomorrow

PEARSON realize | Go online to access your interactive digital lesson.

Chapter 5

TEKS Practice

TEKS 3.B, 14.C

4. Write numbers. Today is November 3.

NOVEMBER

SUNDAY	MONDAY	TUESDAY	WEDNESDAY	TUESDAY	FRIDAY	SATURDAY
	1	2	3	4	5	6
7	8	9	10	11	12	13
14	15	16	17	18	19	20
21	22	23	24	25	26	27
28	29	30				

What was yesterday?

November __________

What will tomorrow be?

November __________

TEKS 2.A

5. Match Draw a line from a name to a matching picture.

George Washington

Christopher Columbus

TEKS 2.A

6. Write P for **patriot.**
Write E for **explorer.**

George Washington  __________

Christopher Columbus __________

Chapter 5

TEKS Practice

TEKS 13.A

7. **Circle** an example of modern technology used at home or in school.

TEKS 13.C

8. **Circle** one of the words that describes modern technology. **Tell** what your life would be like without it.

computer car

telephone bus

my Story Book

Texas Essential Knowledge and Skills

SS 15.B Create visuals, including pictures.

ELA 13 Students use elements of the writing process (planning, drafting) to compose text.

Draw one way people traveled long ago.
Then **draw** one way you travel today.

Teaching Note: Read the prompts. Then brainstorm modes of transportation, past and present. List ideas under the labels of "Long Ago" and "Today." Then have children complete the activity. After the drawing is finished, ask children to describe their pictures.

Atlas

The United States of America, Political

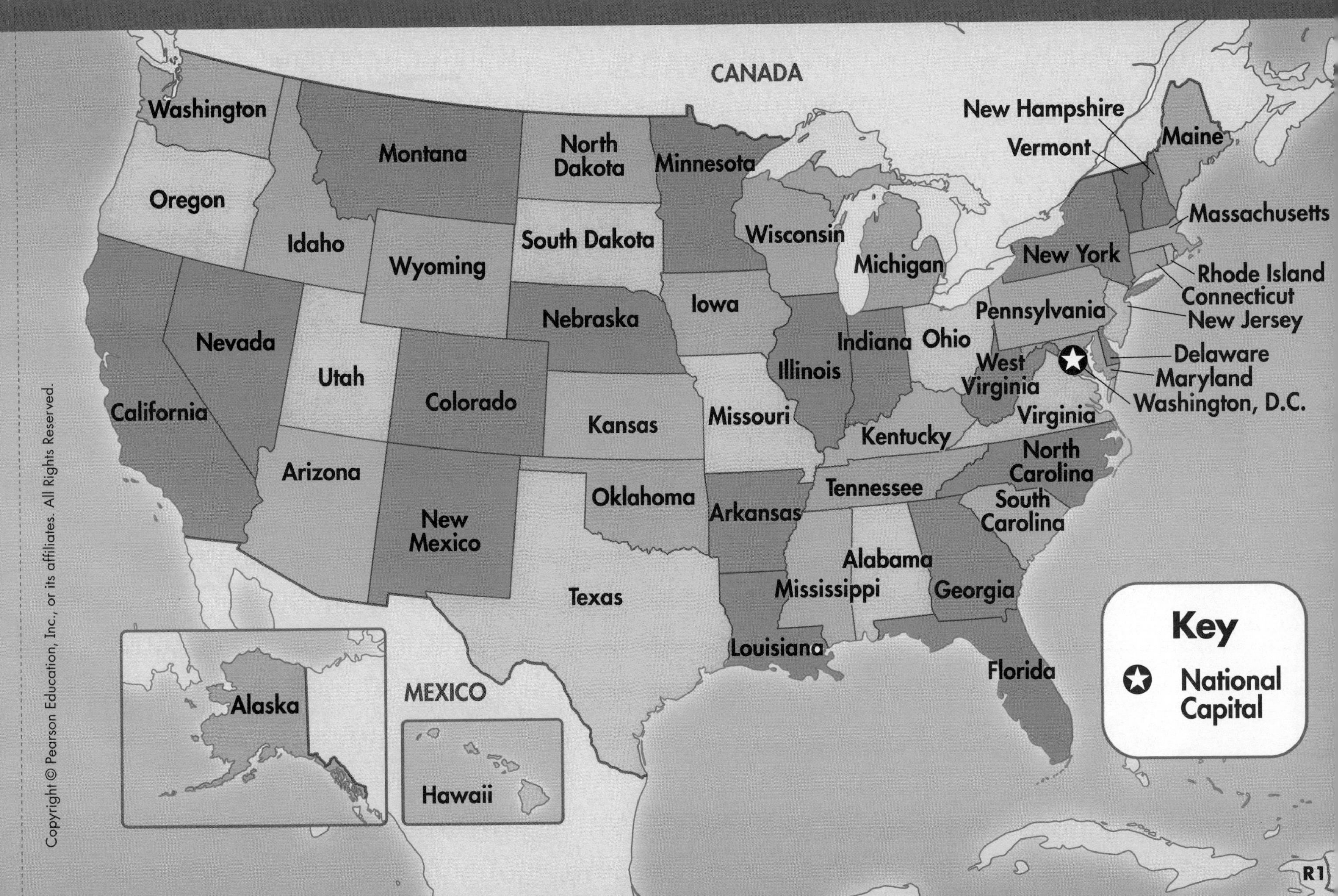

The United States of America, Physical

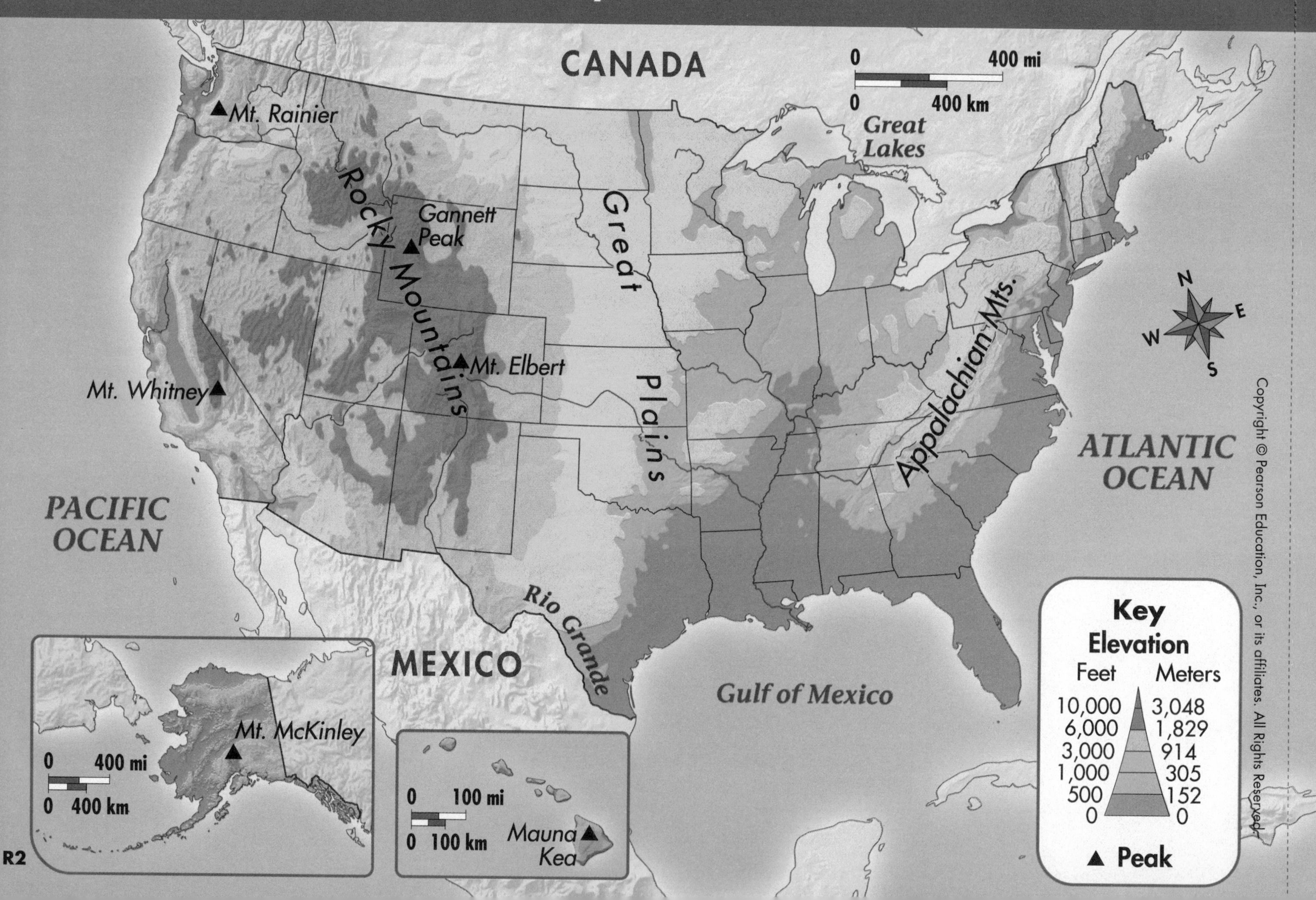

The World

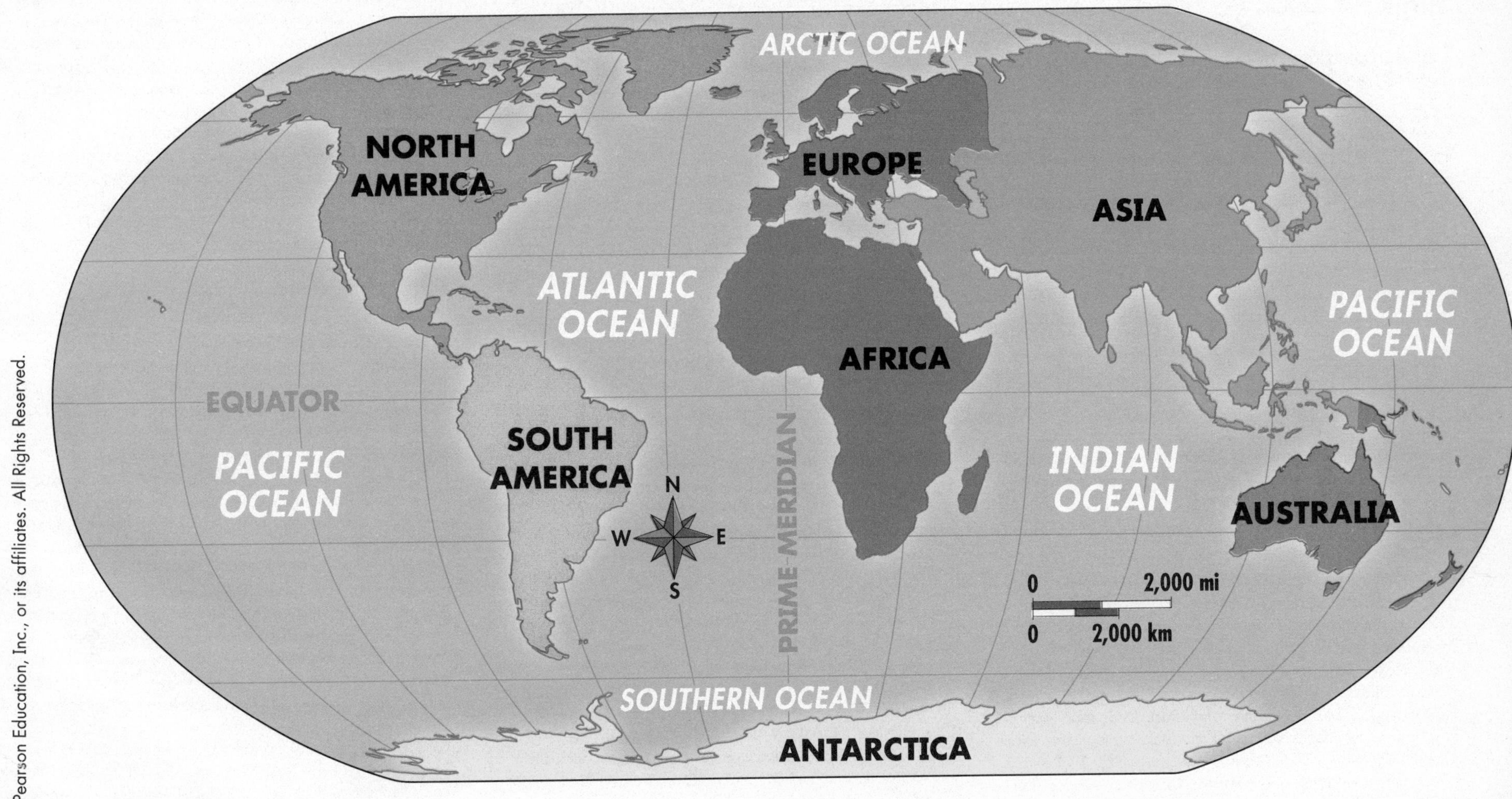
ARCTIC OCEAN
NORTH AMERICA
EUROPE
ASIA
ATLANTIC OCEAN
PACIFIC OCEAN
AFRICA
EQUATOR
SOUTH AMERICA
PACIFIC OCEAN
PRIME MERIDIAN
INDIAN OCEAN
AUSTRALIA
N
W
E
S
0
2,000 mi
0
2,000 km
SOUTHERN OCEAN
ANTARCTICA

Credits

Text Acknowledgments

Grateful acknowledgement is made to the following for copyrighted material:

Page 8 Song "Texas, Our Texas," music by William J. Marsh, lyrics by Gladys Yoakum Wright & William J. Marsh.

Maps

XNR Productions, Inc.

Photographs

Photo locators denoted as follows: Top (T), Center (C), Bottom (B), Left (L), Right (R), Background (Bkgd)

Cover

Front Cover Top Row: Monarch butterfly, Bastos/Fotolia; Second Row: (L) Statue of Liberty, DK Images; Third Row: (L) Subway shuttle in Dallas, Amar and Isabelle Guillen - Guillen Photo LLC/Alamy; (C) American flag, iStockphoto/Thinkstock; (R) Soccer ball, Hemera/Thinkstock; Bottom Row: (C) Turtle, Amar and Isabelle Guillen - Guillen Photo LLC/Alamy. **Back Cover** (CC) Firefighter, Tom Tracy Photography/Alamy; (CR) United States penny, United States Mint; (BL) Crossing guard, Andersen Ross/Blend Images/Getty Images; (BR) Boy and map, Per-Anders Pettersson/Contributor/Getty Images.

Text

Celebrate Texas and the Nation

001: Tips Images/Tips Italia Srl a socio unico/Alamy; 002: Onur Ersin/Shutterstock; 004: Hulton Archive/Archive Photos/Getty Images; 004: University of Texas at San Antonio Libraries Special Collections; 006: Tips Images/Tips Italia Srl a socio unico/Alamy; 007: cphotos100/Fotolia

Chapter 01

009: Ariel Skelley/Getty Images; 010: Pearson Education; 012: Bob Daemmrich/Alamy; 012: Cynthia Farmer/Shutterstock; 012: iStockphoto/Thinkstock; 012: Jupiterimages/Thinkstock; 012: Pearson Education; 013: Ariel Skelley/Getty Images; 013: Pearson Education; 014: Ariel Skelley/Getty Images; 014: JLP/Jose L. Pelaez/Corbis; 014: Jupiterimages/Thinkstock; 014: MaszaS/Shutterstock; 015: Jamie Grill/Getty Images; 015: Pearson Education; 023: Brand X Pictures/Thinkstock; 023: Brian Summers/First Light/Glow Images; 023: paul mansfield photography/Flickr Open/Getty Images; 025: Creasource/Corbis; 025: Shutterstock; 026: Lawrence Migdale/Getty Images; 026: Pearson Education; 027: Monkey Business Images/Shutterstock; 028: Huntstock, Inc/Alamy; 028: John Lund/Marc Romanelli/Blend Images/Vetta/Getty Images; 028: Michelle D. Bridwell/PhotoEdit; 031: Goodshoot/Thinkstock; 031: Jupiterimages/Thinkstock; 031: Susan Montgomery/Shutterstock; 032: Dorling Kindersley, Ltd; 032: Klaus Nigge/National Geographic Stock; 032: Richard Fitzer/Shutterstock; 032: Stockbyte/Thinkstock; 032: Susan Montgomery/Shutterstock

Chapter 02

037: Ariel Skelley/Blend Images/Getty Images; 038: Pearson Education; 040: Amanda Flagg/Shutterstock; 040: Dorling Kindersley,Ltd; 040: Hemera/Thinkstock; 040: iStockphoto/Thinkstock; 040: Jose Inc/Blend Images/Photolibrary; 041: Anetta/Shutterstock; 041: Dorling Kindersley,Ltd; 041: iStockphoto/Thinkstock; 042: Galushko Sergey/Shutterstock; 042: iStockphoto/Thinkstock; 042: Petrenko Andriy/Shutterstock; 042: Roman Sigaev/Shutterstock; 045: Dorling Kindersley,Ltd; 045: Robert Marmion/Alamy; 049: Hill Street Studios/Blend Images/Getty Images; 049: Kraig Scarbinsky/Getty Images; 049: Hill Street Studios/Blend Images/Getty Images; 049: Joe Sohm/Visions of America, LLC/Alamy; 050: Africa Studio/Fotolia; 050: mangostock/Shutterstock; 050: Tom Tracy Photography/Alamy; 051: BananaStock/Thinkstock; 053: Pavel L Photo and Video/Shutterstock; 053: Stephen Coburn/Fotolia; 053: taelove7/Shutterstock; 055: Blend Images/Alamy; 055: moodboard/Photolibrary; 056: Blend Images/DreamPictures/Getty Images; 056: Comstock/Thinkstock; 056: Ikonoklast Fotografie/Shutterstock; 056: konoklast Fotografie/Shutterstock; 056: Ragnar Schmuck/fStop/Photolibrary

Chapter 03

061: Ariel Skelley/Getty Images; 062: Pearson Education; 064: Aurora Photos/Alamy; 064: Jupiterimages/Thinkstock; 064: Kevin Fleming/Corbis; 064: Per-Anders Pettersson/Contributor/Getty Images News/Getty Images; 064: spacephotos com/AGE Fotostock; 068: iStockphoto/Thinkstock; 073: JLP/Jose L. Pelaez/Corbis; 075: Aurora Photos/Alamy; 075: Jupiterimages/Photos.com/Thinkstock; 075: Kevin Fleming/Corbis; 075: spacephotos com/AGE Fotostock; 078: Aurora Photos/Alamy; 078: Dorling Kindersley Ltd; 078: Hemera/Thinkstock; 078: Sensi Images/Alamy; 079: Jupiterimages/Thinkstock; 079: Steve Skjold/Alamy; 079: Stockbyte/Getty Images; 083: Alan Novelli/Alamy; 083: Charlie Waite/Getty Images; 083: John W Banagan/Iconica/Getty Images; 083: robyelo357/Fotolia; 083: Spyros Bourboulis/First Light/Corbis; 083: Wally Stemberger/Shutterstock; 085: Alaska Stock/Alamy; 085: Bill Brooks/Alamy; 085: Joshua Roper/Alamy; 085: Karen Kasmauski/Science Faction/Corbis; 085: National Geographic/Getty Images; 085: vilainecrevette/Fotolia; 086: Chel Beeson/Stockbyte/Getty Images; 086: DreamPictures/Photodisc/Getty Images; 086: Mira/Alamy

Chapter 04

091: Justin Guariglia/Getty Images; 092: Pearson Education; 094: Asia Images/Getty Images; 094: Bill Bachmann/Alamy; 094: Bill Bachmann/Alamy; 094: Blend Images/SuperStock; 094: Blend Images/SuperStock; 094: Comstock/Thinkstock; 094: Phil Date/Shutterstock; 097: BananaStock/Thinkstock; 097: moodboard/Corbis; 099: Andy Dean/Fotolia; 099: Golden Pixels LLC/Alamy; 099: Golden Pixels/Alamy; 099: Monkey Business Images/Shutterstock; 099: Ocean/Corbis; 101: frans lemmens/Alamy; 101: Monkey Business Images/Shutterstock; 101: Ryan McVay/Getty Images; 101: Stewart Cohen/Pam Ostrow/Blend Images/Getty Images; 107: cheng/Shutterstock; 107: Lori Martin/fotolia; 107: Steve Geer/Getty Images; 107: TaurusPhotography/Alamy; 109: BananaStock/Thinkstock; 109: Brand X Pictures/Jupiterimages/Thinkstock; 109: Comstock/Thinkstock; 111: Blend Images/Superstock; 111: David Grossman/Alamy; 111: gary718/Shutterstock; 111: spiritofamerica/Fotolia; 113: Lawrence Migdale/Getty Images; 113: Mark Ralston/AFP/Getty Images; 113: Patrik Giardino/Blend Images/Getty Images; 113: Vidler/Mauritius/SuperStock; 115: Thinkstock Images; 116: Bill Bachmann/Alamy; 116: Golden Pixels LLC/Alamy; 116: Hugh Sitton/Corbis; 116: Pearson Education; 117: Banana Stock/PhotoLibrary; 117: Blend Images/SuperStock; 117: JGI/Tom Grill/Blend Images/Corbis; 117: Ronnie Kaufman/Corbis

Chapter 05

119: H. Armstrong Roberts/Retrofile/Getty Images; 119: Jupiterimages/Comstock/Thinkstock; 119: Jupiterimages/Thinkstock; 120: Pearson Education; 122: AP Images; 122: Cameilia/Shutterstock; 122: George Marks/Retrofile/Getty Images; 122: Jamie Grill/Blend Images/JGI/Corbis; 122: Kenneth Sponsier/Shutterstock; 123: Gelpi/Shutterstock; 123: iStockphoto/Thinkstock; 123: Photodisc/Getty Images/Thinkstock; 123: Ryan McVay/The Image Bank/Getty Images; 124: Anetta/Shutterstock; 124: Hemera/Thinkstock; 124: iStockphoto/Thinkstock; 124: Vereshchagin Dmitry/Shutterstock; 127: Pearson Education; 128: Pearson Education; 129: Hemera/Thinkstock; 129: JGI/Blend Images/Corbis; 131: Hemera/Thinkstock; 131: iStockphoto/Thinkstock; 131: Ljupco Smokovski/Shutterstock; 132: BananaStock/Thinkstock; 132: Tony Campbell/Shutterstock; 133: Hemera/Thinkstock; 133: Image Source/Getty Images; 133: Images.com/Alamy; 134: Comstock/Getty Images; 134: frescomovie/Shutterstock; 134: Hemera/Thinkstock; 135: Ariel Skelley/Getty Images; 136: Denis Felix/Taxi/Getty Images; 136: Gary S Chapman/Stone/Getty Images; 136: Jon Feingersh/SuperStock; 137: Georgios Kollidas/Fotolia; 139: AP Images; 141: Hemera/Thinkstock; 141: SuperStock/Getty Images; 142: Hemera/Thinkstock; 142: iStockphoto/Thinkstock; 142: LAMB/Alamy; 145: Andy Dean/Fotolia; 145: SSPL/Hulton Archive/Getty Images; 146: David Brimm/Shutterstock; 146: ene/Shutterstock; 146: iStockphoto/Thinkstock; 146: only4denn/Fotolia